Drupal 8 Blueprints

Step along the creation of 7 professional-grade Drupal sites

Alex Burrows

BIRMINGHAM - MUMBAI

Drupal 8 Blueprints

First published: September 2017

Production reference: 1150917

Published by Packt Publishing Ltd.
Livery Place
35 Livery Street
Birmingham
B3 2PB, UK.

ISBN 978-1-78588-756-7

www.packtpub.com

Credits

Author
Alex Burrows

Reviewer
John Bloomfield

Commissioning Editor
Amarabha Banerjee

Acquisition Editor
Siddharth Mandal

Content Development Editor
Aditi Gour

Technical Editor
Shweta Jadhav

Copy Editor
Shaila Kusanale

Project Coordinator
Ritika Manoj

Proofreader
Safis Editing

Indexer
Mariammal Chettiyar

Graphics
Jason Monteiro

Production Coordinator
Shantanu Zagade

About the Author

Alex Burrows is a web developer who specializes in Drupal and is based in Surrey, UK. He is the technical director of a UK-based agency called Digidrop, also based in Surrey, UK. He set up Digidrop with his best friend, Matthias, in 2017, and the company is growing fast.

He has worked with Drupal since 2008 and has worked on some well-known brands and large-scale projects; he is also very active within the Drupal community and attends every European and North American Drupalcon, where he is a mentor as well.

He is also one of the directors of Drupalcamp London CIC, which has been running since 2013, and he has been involved in the organization and its running since the beginning. Each year, it is becoming a bigger, better, and more popular event, and it has been marked as the second biggest Drupalcamp in the world.

Writing this book was both an achievement and challenge I wanted to do. I would like to thank my parents and brother, best friends Matthias Sparshot, Bianca Sparshot, and Godson Georges, as well as all my family and friends for giving me the time to write this. I would also like to thank my technical reviewer, John Bloomfield, who I've worked with and know well, Matt Glaman for his encouragement and support throughout, and everyone at Packt, especially Aditi Gour (content editor), Shweta Jadhav (technical editor), and Siddharth Mandal (acquisition editor).

Finally, as this book was in its final review stage, I reached my nine-year Drupal anniversary.

Thank you for buying this book. You can follow me on Twitter as well at @aburrows.

About the Reviewer

John Bloomfield is a web developer who lives in Oxfordshire, UK. He has been working in the web industry since 2002. He specializes in Drupal and is the technical director of JRB Digital Ltd.

He has worked with Drupal since 2009 and has worked on some large-enterprise projects with BBC Worldwide, PwC, BrightLemon, the Australian government, and CTI Digital.

At BBC Worldwide, he was part of the team that created BBC Store and also worked on the BBC Top Gear and BBC Good Food websites.

I have worked with Alex on some large-enterprise projects at PwC and BrightLemon and know him well. His Drupal knowledge is of a high standard, and I thoroughly enjoyed reviewing this book. Thanks to Alex for asking me to be his technical reviewer.

www.Packtpub.com

For support files and downloads related to your book, please visit www.PacktPub.com. Did you know that Packt offers eBook versions of every book published, with PDF and ePub files available? You can upgrade to the eBook version at www.PacktPub.com and as a print book customer, you are entitled to a discount on the eBook copy. Get in touch with us at service@packtpub.com for more details.

At www.PacktPub.com, you can also read a collection of free technical articles, sign up for a range of free newsletters and receive exclusive discounts and offers on Packt books and eBooks.

https://www.packtpub.com/mapt

Get the most in-demand software skills with Mapt. Mapt gives you full access to all Packt books and video courses, as well as industry-leading tools to help you plan your personal development and advance your career.

Why subscribe?

- Fully searchable across every book published by Packt
- Copy and paste, print, and bookmark content
- On demand and accessible via a web browser

Customer Feedback

Thanks for purchasing this Packt book. At Packt, quality is at the heart of our editorial process. To help us improve, please leave us an honest review on this book's Amazon page at www.amazon.in/dp/1785887564.

If you'd like to join our team of regular reviewers, you can email us at customerreviews@packtpub.com. We award our regular reviewers with free eBooks and videos in exchange for their valuable feedback. Help us be relentless in improving our products!

Table of Contents

Preface

Drupal is a very powerful open source content management system (over 1,000,000 websites run on Drupal). There have been eight versions of Drupal, and in my opinion, the latest is the greatest by far. Drupal 8 has been been redeveloped from the core to have more features, which means that far less coding is needed than before. This book is for anyone, especially those new to Drupal. It will guide you through making seven types of website without much custom code at all. The following is a quote from the official website of Drupal:

> *"What is Drupal? Drupal is the #1 platform for web content management among global enterprises, governments, higher education institutions, and NGOs. Flexible and highly scalable, Drupal publishes a single website or shares content in multiple languages across many devices. Technology and business leaders transform content management into powerful digital solutions with Drupal... backed by one of the world's most innovative open source communities."*

What this book covers

Chapter 1, *Introduction and Getting Set Up*, shows how to get started with development locally and how to get set up for Drupal.

Chapter 2, *Telling Your Own Story with Drupal*, describes how to create your very own blog.

Chapter 3, *Get Fundraising with Drupal*, is about creating a fundraising website that donations can be made to.

Chapter 4, *Recruit Using Drupal*, presents a way to show the jobs that are available and apply for jobs.

Chapter 5, *List Properties with Drupal*, explores how to create a website showing properties for sale.

Chapter 6, *Express Your Event with Drupal*, focuses on how to create a website for an event, and show sessions, tracks, and a schedule.

Chapter 7, *Get Teaching with Drupal*, covers the use of videos to teach.

Chapter 8, *Go Static with Drupal*, outlines how to use Drupal to work with a static frontend.

What you need for this book

To get started with Drupal, you will require a local development environment, as we will cover in `Chapter 1`, *Introduction and Getting Set Up*.

In order to create code, you will need a text editor. The recommended ones are as follows:

- PHPStorm--`https://www.jetbrains.com/phpstorm/download`
- Sublime Text 3--`https://www.sublimetext.com/3`
- Netbeans--`https://netbeans.org/features/index.html`

Who this book is for

The book is for people who have used or installed Drupal before, have some understanding of how websites work, and have some PHP knowledge.

It is a step-by-step guide on creating seven types of website, exploring how powerful Drupal 8 is without having to write too much custom code.

Conventions

In this book, you will find a number of text styles that distinguish between different kinds of information. Here are some examples of these styles and an explanation of their meaning.

Code words in text, database table names, folder names, filenames, file extensions, pathnames, dummy URLs, user input, and Twitter handles are shown as follows: "To get panels, simply type `composer require drupal/panels drupal/page_manager`."

A block of code is set as follows:

```
name: Blueprint
description: Bespoke theme for Drupal 8 Blueprints
type: theme
core: 8.x
base theme: bootstrap
# Regions
```

Any command-line input or output is written as follows:

```
drush dl bootstrap
```

New terms and **important words** are shown in bold. Words that you see on the screen, for example, in menus or dialog boxes, appear in the text like this: "Select **System info** from the **Administration** panel."

Warnings or important notes appear in a box like this.

Tips and tricks appear like this.

Reader feedback

Feedback from our readers is always welcome. Let us know what you think about this book-what you liked or disliked. Reader feedback is important for us as it helps us develop titles that you will really get the most out of.

To send us general feedback, simply e-mail feedback@packtpub.com, and mention the book's title in the subject of your message.

If there is a topic that you have expertise in and you are interested in either writing or contributing to a book, see our author guide at www.packtpub.com/authors .

Customer support

Now that you are the proud owner of a Packt book, we have a number of things to help you to get the most from your purchase.

Downloading the color images of this book

We also provide you with a PDF file that has color images of the screenshots/diagrams used in this book. The color images will help you better understand the changes in the output. You can download this file from
https://www.packtpub.com/sites/default/files/downloads/Drupal8Blueprints_ColorI mages.pdf.

Errata

Although we have taken every care to ensure the accuracy of our content, mistakes do happen. If you find a mistake in one of our books-maybe a mistake in the text or the code-we would be grateful if you could report this to us. By doing so, you can save other readers from frustration and help us improve subsequent versions of this book. If you find any errata, please report them by visiting http://www.packtpub.com/submit-errata, selecting your book, clicking on the **Errata Submission Form** link, and entering the details of your errata. Once your errata are verified, your submission will be accepted and the errata will be uploaded to our website or added to any list of existing errata under the Errata section of that title.

To view the previously submitted errata, go to
https://www.packtpub.com/books/content/support and enter the name of the book in the search field. The required information will appear under the **Errata** section.

Piracy

Piracy of copyrighted material on the Internet is an ongoing problem across all media. At Packt, we take the protection of our copyright and licenses very seriously. If you come across any illegal copies of our works in any form on the Internet, please provide us with the location address or website name immediately so that we can pursue a remedy.

Please contact us at copyright@packtpub.com with a link to the suspected pirated material.

We appreciate your help in protecting our authors and our ability to bring you valuable content.

Questions

If you have a problem with any aspect of this book, you can contact us at questions@packtpub.com, and we will do our best to address the problem.

1
Introduction and Getting Set Up

Welcome to Drupal 8 Blueprints!

I'm *Alex Burrows,* and I'll be your guide for this journey through building websites using Drupal 8.

Firstly, this book is aimed at beginner to intermediate-level developers. You'll need an understanding of how websites work and some PHP knowledge, as we will later delve into writing some custom modules, but mostly, this book will use Drupal's powerful configuration.

Throughout the book, we will go over things we covered earlier; however, the aim is to understand the basics and, if at any time, you become unsure, review the chapter where it was covered.

We will cover the following to get you ready to build websites using Drupal 8 first:

- Setting up for local development:
    - Setting up on Windows
    - Setting up on macOS
- What is SSH?
- Our great development tools:
    - Homebrew
    - iTerm
    - Oh MyZsh

- Setting up our local development environment:
    - Native
    - Acquia DevDesktop
    - Vagrant
    - Docker
- Terminology
- Drush and Drupal Console
- Installing Drupal:
    - Getting our basic site
    - Drupal core structure
    - Downloading modules and themes
    - Using themes
- Get involved with Drupal

So, get ready to learn and build some awesome websites using Drupal 8!

Setting up for local development

As we will start a site that requires PHP and MySQL to run, we need to set up a local development environment.

There are many ways that this can be achieved; the most favorable ones are Vagrant and Docker. Oh, and of course, if you're developing a Drupal site, Acquia DevDesktop is a good option as well. This book is highly focused on you developing Drupal on a macOS; however, there are other explanations on how to do this on Windows, and Acquia DevDesktop works on Windows. I will explain how to set up shell on Windows as well, but the only local tool I recommend for now is Acquia DevDesktop as I have had many issues with Vagrant on a Windows machine.

Setting up on Windows

Firstly, since Windows is not a Unix-based operating system, we need to install Git for Windows (`https://git-for-windows.github.io`). This includes setting up your machine with Git Bash, Git Gui, and Shell Integration.

However, as for Windows 10, it allows Bash (`https://msdn.microsoft.com/en-gb/commandline/wsl/about`), and the website--`https://www.howtogeek.com/249966/how-to-install-and-use-the-linux-bash-shell-on-windows-10`--has some great tutorials that explain how to set up.

Setting up on macOS

As a developer, I love macOS, because for me it just works. I have multiple tools that I use and highly recommend, which I will go into more depth further on in this chapter.

What is SSH?

Secure Socket Shell, otherwise known as (**SSH**), allows us to access our directories and files on our operating system, whether it's on our local development environment or our live web server.

In order to do this on macOS, we need to launch the Terminal application. On Windows, we can use the Bash application that was explained earlier.

We can execute commands with SSH to do this; for example, we can change to another folder/directory using the following:

```
cd mydirectory
```

Alternatively, we can create a new folder/directory using this:

```
mkdir mydirectory
```

These are just some examples of SSH commands, and I encourage you to take a look into this.

When we are doing this development, especially where we are using dynamic code such as PHP, we need to be able to add other tools using the command line.

Our great development tools for macOS

There are some very important tools that I use for development. These not only make my processes quicker, but they also allow me to enhance my development environment to how I need it.

An example of this is that if I might need to install an add-on quickly, I can do this using Homebrew.

Some of the helpful add-ons I use are as follows:

- Homebrew
- iTerm
- Oh My Zsh

Homebrew

The first important tool is HomeBrew (no, it's not teaching you how to make some alcohol at home). It is a fantastic addition to the shell that allows us to execute and install packages very easily.

If you go to `https://brew.sh`, you can copy and paste into Terminal and away you go, with very simple commands, such as the following:

```
brew install curl
```

What the preceding command will do is to download and install the `curl` package for us. This is just an example of what it does.

iTerm

As it says on their website:

> *"iTerm2 is a replacement for Terminal and the successor to iTerm. It works on Macs with macOS 10.8 or newer. iTerm2 brings the Terminal into the modern age with features you never knew but always wanted."*

This allows us to make our experience using the Terminal a lot better (`https://www.iterm2.com`).

Oh My Zsh

This allows us to run commands and shortcuts. We don't have to type out full commands, as we did earlier, and we can use our own commands and shortcuts to achieve tasks a lot quicker (`http://ohmyz.sh`).

Setting up our local development environment

As with anything, there are a lot of choices for local environments. These are just samples of the ones that are there and what they do.

Native

As macOS is built on a Unix framework, you can use this entirely to run your local host, and its just a case of editing some files on your mac and changing them. There is some great documentation on this at (`http://php.net/manual/en/install.macosx.bundled.php`).

Acquia DevDesktop

This is an all-inclusive application that allows you to get started and set up with making your Drupal websites locally. We will indeed use this for the entire book. It creates the URL for your local website as well as the database and Drupal core.

We use this at Drupal events, and we are mentoring people new to Drupal (`https://www.acquia.com/gb/products-services/dev-desktop`).

The next two require VirtualBox. This allows us to create virtual machines on both mac and Windows. From here, we can create our separate machines and download OS images that will allow us to install Linux OS, or if you have a Windows disk, you can install this (`https://www.virtualbox.org/wiki/Downloads`).

Vagrant

This allows you to create and define what your virtual machine will have and require (`https://vagrantup.com`).

> Vagrant provides the same easy workflow regardless of your role as a developer, operator, or designer. It leverages a declarative configuration file that describes all your software requirements, packages, operating system configuration, users, and more.

One great VM to use for Drupal can be found at (`https://www.drupalvm.com`).

I personally use this for all local development.

Docker

This again allows you to create and define what your development environment will have, but it uses a thing called containers to achieve this (`https://www.docker.com`).

Using containers, everything required to make a piece of software run is packaged into isolated containers. Unlike VMs, containers do not bundle a full operating system; only libraries and settings required to make the software work are needed. This makes for efficient, lightweight, self-contained systems and guarantees that the software will always run the same, regardless of where it's deployed.

Terminology

Within Drupal and the community, there is some terminology that we use; the following are some of them along with what they mean:

- **Content type**: This is an entity type, and the individual content types within it are called bundles; in this case, we have a basic page bundle and an article bundle by default
- **Node**: A node is a piece of content; this is usually within a content type, and a content type is indeed an entity type
- **Taxonomy**: This is another name for a category, so we can distinguish types of content based on the category name; this is usually used for filtering content
- **Themes**: This is what makes our site look the way it is
- **Modules**: Another name for a plugin that adds functionality to Drupal

Drush and Drupal Console

In Drupal, we have some powerful tools that allow us to run commands to execute on our website. This is all run using the command line; an example of this is that we can download themes and modules directly off `Drupal.org` just by running one command.

Both Drush and Drupal Console are very similar in what they do, and it's down to preference as to which you prefer. For this book, we will use Drupal Console.

Installing Drupal

For now, we will just install Drupal using DevDesktop; however, we will change how we do this later on.

To do this, open up DevDesktop, then bottom left click on +, and then select **New Drupal Site**. Then, once the popup appears, click on **Install** in the row that Drupal 8 is in. This will appear with a popup:

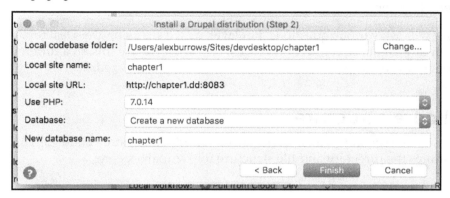

Fig 1.0: Install Drupal 8.x site

Once this is done, click on the **Local site**:

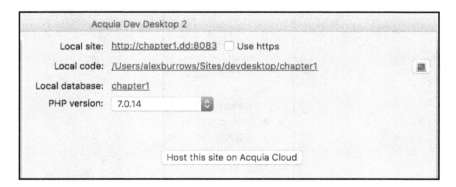

Fig 1.1

In the pereceding *Fig 1.1*, we can now get our Drupal site up and running.

We can see four lines of content:

- **Local site**: This is the URL that our website is accessible on locally
- **Local code**: This is where our code is currently located; further along, there is a little square button on the right, which launches a Terminal window
- **Local database**: This is the name of our database
- **PHP version**: This is the version of PHP being used

Getting our basic site

Now that we have downloaded and set up our Drupal site to work on our local environment, let's begin installing our site.

The installer will ask various questions; however, as we are using DevDesktop, we don't need to enter any database connection details, but when we use this on a different local environment or even our production environment, it is all required.

Drupal core structure

In Drupal, we have several locations where our contrib and custom code go. The following figure illustrates the directory and file structure for Drupal 8.x core:

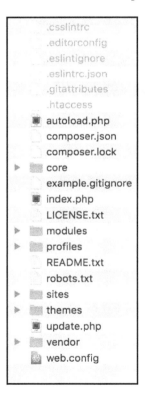

All custom and contrib items need to go into either modules, profiles, or themes.

The recommended structure inside these directories to add the `contrib` and `custom` directories. Consider the following examples:

- Modules:
  - `/modules/contrib`
  - `/modules/custom`
- Profiles:
  - `/profiles/contrib`
  - `/profiles/custom`
- Themes:
  - `/themes/contrib`
  - `/themes/custom`

There are other key directories here that don't need to be touched, but there is also a `sites` directory, which contains our sites configuration to access the database, files storage, libraries, and services.

Downloading modules and themes

Once our site is installed, we need to download our base theme for our site, so we can do the following to get modules or themes:

- Download directly from `Drupal.org`

  `https://drupal.org/project/{module or theme name}`

- Download using Drush

  `drush dl project`, **for example**, `drush dl bootstrap`

- Download using Drupal console

  `drupal:install project`

Using themes

With Drupal, we can start a site without writing any code for a theme, as Drupal core comes with the following accessible themes:

- Bartik
- Seven
- Stark

Apart from these three, there are two others that are used as the entire base of Drupal core-- Stable and Classy.

Classy is a subtheme of stable, makes Drupal look the way it does, and adds classes.

However, we want to get started with our own theme. So to do this, we need to open Terminal. As stated earlier, the button in DevDesktop on the right-hand side will launch our Terminal window.

Once this is open, we can download our modules and themes straight into our Drupal site. For this book, we will use Bootstrap as our base theme and then create our own theme:

```
drush dl bootstrap
```

This will download the Bootstrap theme (https://drupal.org/project/bootstrap) into our themes directory.

Now that we have Bootstrap downloaded, let's create a really basic theme so that we can add onto it later on. Inside our /themes/custom directory, create a new directory called blueprint.

This is where our custom theme will be stored; inside this, we have the ability to add our frontend structure, which includes our templates, CSS, and Javascript.

Start by creating a file called blueprint.info.yml; note that we have it structured as THEMENAME.info.yml.

In Drupal 8.x, we have adopted the use of YAML files, and you will note that all configuration in Drupal uses this format.

blueprint.info.yml

```
name: Blueprint
description: Bespoke theme for Drupal 8 Blueprints
type: theme
core: 8.x
base theme: bootstrap
# Regions
```

What this does is to tell Drupal: *Hey I'm a new theme, this is what I do*. It's set out like this:

- **Name**: This is what we are calling our theme, following the same name we have given to our themes directory.
- **Description**: This is a simple description of the theme, and it shows in the Drupal admin interface.
- **Type**: This is saying that this is for a theme; if it was for a module, it would be module instead.
- **Core**: As this is for Drupal 8, we need to specify that it is for Drupal 8.x.
- **Base theme**: We are leveraging our theme files, styles, JavaScript, and templates off of the bootstrap library. This, of course, can be based on any other theme.

Now that we have done this, we are ready to start making a Drupal site and add it to our custom blueprint theme later on.

Getting involved with Drupal

Before we continue, it is recommended that you register at `Drupal.org` and set up a profile; this will help you vastly and will allow you to ask questions on `Drupal.org`, fix bugs, submit bugs, and become part of a fantastic community.

Within the Drupal community, we have two sayings:

Come for the code, stay for the community.

There's a module for that!

Let's get Drupal started!

So, now that we have set up our first Drupal site, we can start with our first website!

 There is a lot to learn in this book, so take your time.

Ensure that you have a caffeinated drink to hand or a glass of water, and enjoy unravelling the true power of Drupal!

2
Telling Your Own Story with Drupal

Latest news is an important part of any website for many businesses. They allow the business to engage with their customers and keep their employees updated. In this chapter, we will create a simple news website using Drupal 8 core functionality. This can also be used as a blog; we're just making it sound exciting and relatable.

This chapter will be a little more in depth in showing how the basic functionality of Drupal works; this will allow quicker development later throughout the book.

We will explore the following topics in the chapter:

- Creating a new content type
- Creating taxonomy terms and associating them to news posts
- Using custom views to display the listing and individual news pages
- Enabling a comment field to allow user comments
- Referencing other news articles on the site
- Setting up restricted articles
- Understanding permissions and roles
- Configuring the editor experience

We will learn how to create a content type and implement the fields required for displaying the news articles; this is more of a refresher on how to do things. We won't go into this much detail on beginner items again. If in doubt, take a relook at this chapter.

We will also create custom view modes for displaying different display types using references from the post, and then finally, move into the theme layer inside twig templates for displaying the content.

Creating the Post content type

In Drupal, we use the terminology of entity, and we have bundles inside an entity. As part of the Drupal core functionality, we have content types, which is in fact an entity type and therefore the Post content type is a bundle.

So, now that we are familiar with some basic Drupal terminology, let's move on to creating our **Post** content type.

If you use the menu at the top and click on **Manage** | **Structure** | **Content Types**, you will be taken to the **Admin** page for **Content types**:

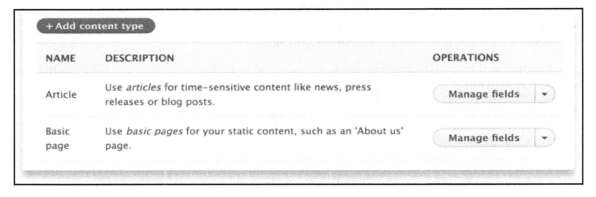

Fig 1.1: The content type management page

By default, we have two content types in a standard Drupal installation (**Basic page** and **Article**). **Article** is pretty much a **Post** content type; however, for this, we shall ignore this and create our own content type entirely from scratch.

To create a new content type, click on **+ Add content type**:

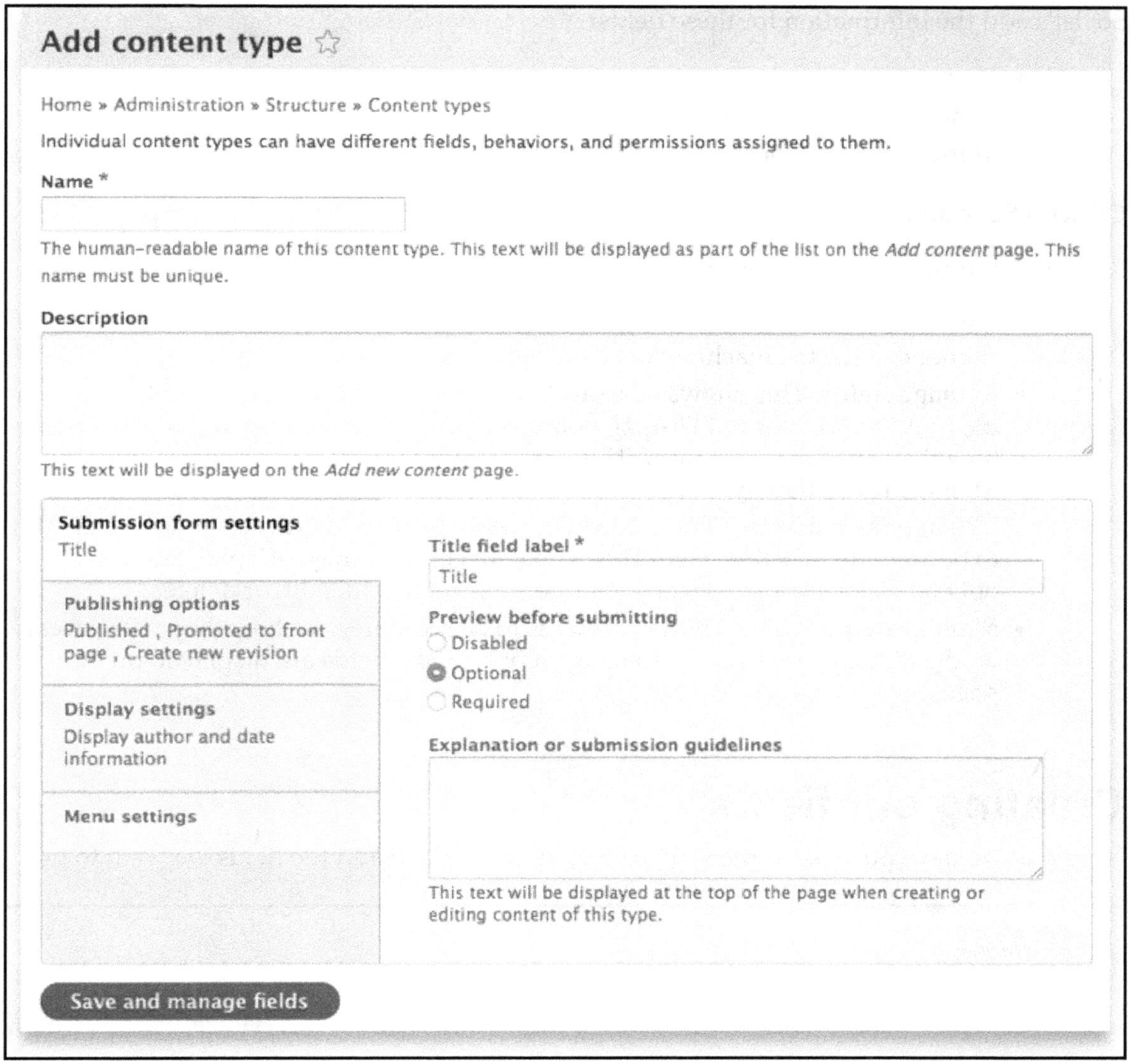

Add content type ☆

Home » Administration » Structure » Content types

Individual content types can have different fields, behaviors, and permissions assigned to them.

Name *

The human-readable name of this content type. This text will be displayed as part of the list on the *Add content* page. This name must be unique.

Description

This text will be displayed on the *Add new content* page.

Submission form settings	**Title field label** *
Title	Title
Publishing options	**Preview before submitting**
Published , Promoted to front page , Create new revision	○ Disabled
	● Optional
	○ Required
Display settings	**Explanation or submission guidelines**
Display author and date information	
Menu settings	
	This text will be displayed at the top of the page when creating or editing content of this type.

Save and manage fields

Fig 1.2: The Add content type page

On this page, we are presented with some fields, which we use to set up how a content type works.

So, let's add the information for these fields:

- **Name**: `Post`
- **Description**: Create a new post to display
- **Menu settings**: Uncheck all available menus

Click on **Save and manage fields**, and we have now started our **Post** content type.

The content type is split into four tabs:

- **Edit**: This allows for the settings we just added to be modified; however, you cannot change the machine name once the content type is created.
- **Manage fields**: This allows us to add/edit/remove fields from the content type. In the previous versions of Drupal, you could move the fields up and down to order how they appear on the form. This is no longer the case and appears under the **Manage form display** tab.
- **Manage form display**: This allows for the fields to be reordered and the formats to be amended for this page. This won't affect the **Manage display** tab. It will only be visible to any user who has permission to add, edit, or delete.
- **Manage display**: This allows the fields to be reordered for how they will appear on the display. It will affect the output of how the fields are displayed on the page.

Creating our fields

Now that we have our **Post** content type created, we need to add the fields we want to use:

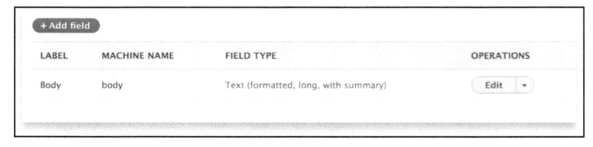

Fig 1.3: Adding fields to content type

In *Fig 1.3*, we can see the layout for adding fields to our content type; we can see that there is already a field called **Body**, which is created by default; the field UI is split into four columns:

- **LABEL**: This is our user-friendly label; when we enter our label, this generates the machine name.
- **MACHINE NAME**: This is the unique name for the field; fields can be reused throughout Drupal, but only one per content type. If we create a field called subtitle, it will generate the machine name as `field_subtitle`; we can, however, override this to name it how we want.
- **FIELD TYPE**: There are various types of fields (text, list, autocomplete, and so on), which are created by plugins, but for now these are the ones we have in Drupal core.
- **OPERATIONS**: These are the features of the field.
- **Edit**: This allows us to edit the basic settings for the field, including label, help text, default value, and any other configuration that is required for the field.
- **Storage settings (Field settings)**: This allows us to set the number of fields we require for this field.

Now that we have a basic understanding of the field system, let's move ahead and create our fields. We do, however, need to categorize the posts after we have created our basic fields so that we get an understanding of what happens; we will then add the categories known in Drupal as taxonomy.

Adding our fields

For our Post to show content, we need to add some fields so that the user can input content. For this, we will have three fields:

- **Post content**: This will be Text (formatted long, with summary)
- **Post comment**: This will be a comment field that utilizes the comment core module
- **Post category**: This will be a taxonomy term reference, which will look up our terms inside our taxonomy

Let's add our first field, **Post content.**

To do this, we click on **+ Add field**; we are then redirected to a page that allows us to configure the field and its type. We are shown **Add a new field** and **Re-use an existing field**. We want to add a new field entirely, so from the drop-down list, let's select Text (formatted long, with summary). As you'll see, when we select this, we are greeted with a new field, **Label**. This field is the name of our field, so we shall use **Post content** as our label. When we enter this into the textfield, we see **Machine name: field_post_content** to the right:

Fig 1.5: Adding field details

In *Fig 1.5*, we can see the field settings all filled in; we are now ready to proceed to the second part of the field configuration:

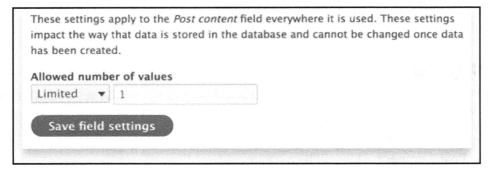

Fig 1.6: Setting number of values

The **Field** API allows us to set as many for a field as we like. If we were to set unlimited, an **Add another** action button appears, and then another field is loaded.

After doing this, when we click on **Save field settings**, we will be taken to another settings page; depending on the type of field, there may be multiple fields for configuration on this field:

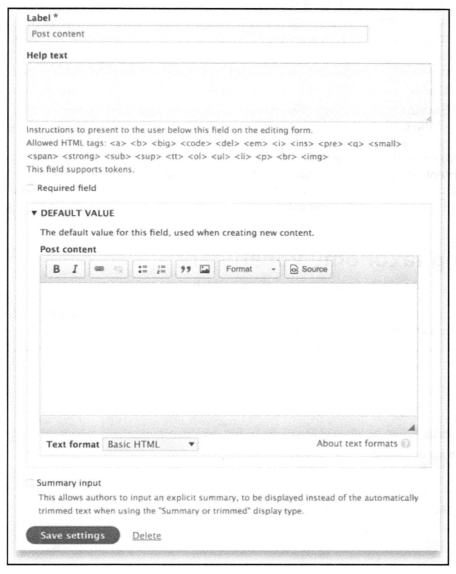

Fig 1.7: Configuring field

In *Fig 1.7*, we can see the following fields:

- **Label**: This appears above the field and will show on the display by default.
- **Help text**: This allows a description to appear beneath the field, and it is used as instructions to the user on what the field requires.
- **Required field**: This allows us to make the field required and use the standard Drupal validation for this type of field; however, we can amend this later, if needed, just by editing the field settings from the **Manage fields** page.
- **Default value**: This will show the same value that can be overridden by the user.
- **Summary input**: This allows authors to show a specific summary of text instead of the basic `trim` function.

As we have created our content field for our post, we now need to add a category selection to this content type. So now, it's time to add our taxonomy; firstly, we need to create a taxonomy vocabulary, and then we can associate our terms to this vocabulary. For this site, we will call our vocabulary "Post category".

Adding taxonomy vocabulary

Now, let's go ahead and create our taxonomy vocabulary.

If you use the menu at the top and click on **Manage | Structure | Taxonomy**, you will be taken to the **Taxonomy** admin page:

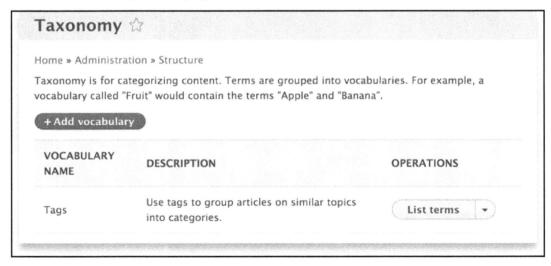

Fig 1.8: Taxonomy administration

In *Fig 1.8*, we can see the layout for adding our vocabulary; we can see that there is already a vocabulary called **Tags**. This will be sufficient for what we need; however, we want to create a new vocabulary to understand how this is done.

Now, if we click on **+ Add vocabulary**, we are taken to another configuration page, where we have two fields:

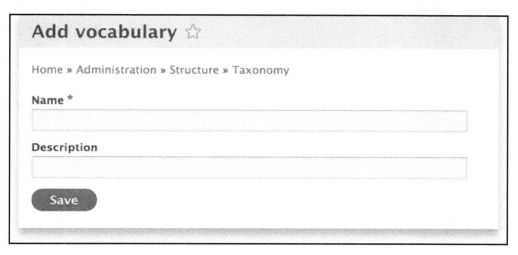

Fig 1.9: The Add vocabulary administration page

We have a **Name** and a **Description** field to enter; the name is what our vocabulary will be called, and the description will appear underneath. After filling in these fields and saving, we are redirected to a page that allows us to add terms.

There are a few ways to create terms by default. We can either add the term directly on this page, or create the terms as we create the content, which is done using an autocomplete text field that will detect an existing term or allow us to create a new one. For now, however, let's create a term manually, and then we can explore how to add a term within our post.

If we click on **+ Add term**, we are redirected to another page that allows us to add details for this term:

Fig 1.10: Term creation page

What we see on this page is as follows:

- **Name**: This is the name of our term
- **Description**: This is a description related to the term
- **Relations**: This allows us to relate the term to other terms
- **URL alias**: This lets us create an SEO-friendly path for the term page; we can automate this later, which we will cover later in the chapter

Once we populate these fields and save them, we will see the same page, but we also see a status message saying we have **Created a new term Drupal** at the top. We can either continue adding terms or return to the vocabulary page. In Drupal taxonomy is an entity type, and again our vocabulary is a bundle. So, we have the power to add fields to our taxonomy terms. We can add any field to this taxonomy term.

Adding fields to our vocabulary

For our category page, we want a nice image to show. So, let's add an image field to this term page. From the current page, click on the breadcrumb **Post category**; this will take us back to the vocabulary page for **Post category**. Now that we are here, we can see tabs across the top. As we saw when we were creating our **Post** content type, we have the following:

- **Manage fields**
- **Manage form display**
- **Manage display**

From here, we can again create and manage the display of the taxonomy term page. Let's add our image upload field.

As we did earlier, we click on **+ Add field** and are again redirected to a configuration page for the field. Let's add our image field; select **Reference | Image**. Then, enter the label of **Post category hero**; this will again generate our machine name for the field. Let's save this and begin configuring the field as we did before; this time the field has a little bit more configuration to do.

On the image field settings, we can see that there is a radio button selected for **Public files**; if we had other file storage setup, such as Amazon S3, then this would show here. However, for now, we are using public files, which will save our images in /sites/default/files.

We then see some fields that allow us to upload a default image, alternative text and title. This will render inside the image when it displays on the site. Let's save this and continue to add the final bit of configuration for this field.

Again, we see fields similar to when we created our **Post content**, but we have some additional ones; we can do the following:

- Set the allowed file extensions
- Set the file directory
- Set the default image
- Set the maximum and minimum image dimensions
- Set the maximum upload size of the file
- Set what type of attribute will be required for the image

We only need to amend the allowed file extensions, as the others will be set to the default settings that are inside Drupal core.

Once we have done this, we can save our new fields and move on to the next part of the build, which is to add the taxonomy to the content type.

Adding more fields

Moving back to our content type, let's incorporate the taxonomy vocabulary we have just created.

We need to go to the **Manage fields** tab inside the Post content type. Once here, we need to add our new field. Let's do that now. Click on **+ Add field**; once again, this will redirect us to a field settings page. For this field, we need to select **Reference | Taxonomy term.** So now, we need to fill in the **Label**; let's call this **Post category**. Once this is done, click on **Save field settings**; now we can fill in our settings for this field.

Leave everything as it is, but under **Reference method,** there is a checkbox labelled **Create referenced entities if they don't already exist,** which basically allows any term that's typed but doesn't already exist to be created. Pretty cool, eh?

Directly beneath that, we have checkboxes for our various vocabularies, as we can see here in *Fig 1.11*:

Fig 1.11

Now that we have done this, let's save our field and go to create our first post!

Creating content

Now is the time to create our very first post!

To do so, we need to do the following:

- Click on **content**, after which we are greeted with our content listing page, which allows us to see all our content on the website ordered by when it was last updated. For now, however, this is showing no entries as we have nothing saved yet.
- To add content, click on **+ Add content**.

We are now taken to another page that shows us the existing content types we can create:

Fig 1.12: The content creation page

If we click on **Post**, we are taken to another page that shows the fields we added earlier:

Fig 1.13: The Create Post page

In *Fig 1.13*, we can see the fields we added, these being **Post content** and **Post category**.

To create our content, we need to fill in the fields, so let's do this now:

- **Post title:** `Our very first news article`
- **Post content:** `We have some exciting news to announce, we've created some content!`; as you can see from this field, we have an editor that allows us to do a variety of things.
- **Post category:** `Up and coming`; if we remember, when we type a taxonomy term that already exists, an autocomplete will run and show a term that is similar to or matches the one we are entering. However, if this term doesn't exist, then it will create it for us!

Other parts of the content creation page are the columns to the right, which are for editorial purposes:

- **Revision**: This allows us to view previously saved content
- **URL path settings**: We can add our own path, but there is a module called **pathauto** that we can use (`https://drupal.org/project/pathauto`)
- **Authoring information**: This will add our username and a timestamp by default; however, we can modify this to show another author and another timestamp
- **Promotion options**: This gives us basic control of how our content is listed; we have two options here:
    - Promoted to front page
    - Sticky at top of lists

Now that we understand how the content creation page works, we can save our content. We can see that there's a **Save and publish** button and to the right-hand side of this button, there is a drop-down arrow; if we click on the arrow, we are shown another option--**Save as unpublished**.

However, we want our first post to be published, so let's do that now:

Fig 1.14

There, you've created your first news article; you'll see `node/1` in the URL after our site URL. This is the default Drupal core naming convention for our content.

Wait, this page looks ugly! We want to change it; we have labels above our content and various other displays. By default, we have view modes of **Default** and **Content**.

Creating our view modes

Our page needs some basic tidying up. Drupal has the **Manage display** for this; by default, without touching any code, we can change the basic look and feel of the page. What view mode allows us to do is to use different "layouts" for our entities and with other modules, such as views. This means that we can show five fields in one view mode, and two in another. Again, this is done without writing any code!

What we will need to do

We want our content to look different to a certain extent; view mode allows us to do this and gives us some good control on the output of our content for different parts of the site.

So, we need to create three view modes:

- **Teaser**: To show the content on the listing page
- **Content**: Our main content to display
- **Related content**: related news articles at the bottom of the content page

How's it done

Moving back to our **Post** content type, we need to modify the way the content is being displayed. To do this, we need to go to the **Manage display** for our content type.

As a shortcut, go to `/admin/structure/types/manage/{content_type}/display` to access this page.

Fig 1.15

In *Fig 1.15* we can see are our fields and **Custom display settings** at the bottom. What we now want to do now is to create a new view mode for **Related content**; to do this, we click on **Custom display settings**, and then we can see the different view modes and **Manage view modes**. This view mode will be available for any content type.

When we are redirected to the view modes configuration page, we can see the following:

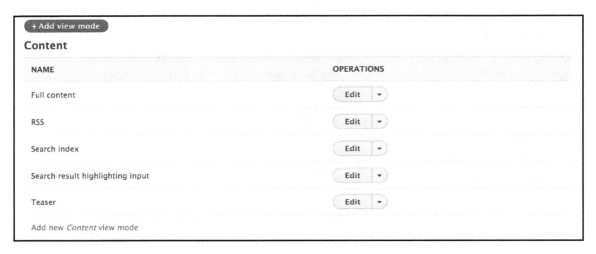

Fig 1.16

If we click on **Add new Content view mod** we can now enter our new view mode and give it a name of **Related content**.

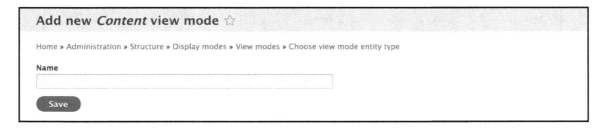

Fig 1.17: Add new Content view mode

In *Fig 1.17*, we will need to enter the **Name**; let's fill this with **Related content** and then click on **Save**. We will now see our view mode appearing in the list on view modes. Now that this has been added, we can enable the view mode for our content type. This now allows us to manage our display in the **Manage display** interface, but first, we need to enable it on the **Manage display** page, so let's move back to this page and enable it. Back on this page, we can see a **Custom display** settings; if we open this up, we can now see our **Related content** view mode, so let's enable that now:

Manage display ☆			
Edit	Manage fields	Manage form display	Manage display
Default	Related content	Teaser	

Fig 1.18

Once this is enabled, we will see it appear beneath the main tabs on the page, as per *Fig 1.18*.

If we click on this, we will be taken to a page that shows the same three fields as we have on default; from here, we can again drag the fields we want in whichever order we want, and this won't affect the other two view modes for our **Post** content type.

Customizing our Post

For our **Related content** view mode, we want to just show the title for now, so if we move our other two fields down into **Disabled**, these won't appear on the view mode, and they won't amend our other view modes. We will use this view mode with the views module so that we can show our content in a different way.

Displaying content with views

Prior to Drupal 8, you would have to download a variety of contrib to use view; however, views is now in Drupal core!

Now that we already have the power of views within, let's go create a view.

Views is used to display content, and can allow us to sort our content in an easy way, therefore reducing the need of custom modules.

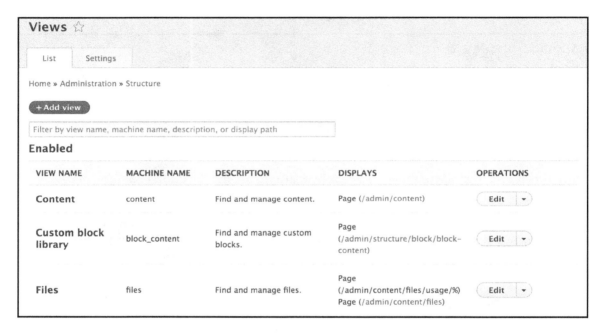

Fig 1.19: Views admin page

If we now go to **Structure | Views**, we will see a page listing content already as per *Fig 1.20*. These are our default views that are part of Drupal core; we can modify them as much as we like. Now, let's create our very first view. For people new to Drupal, views can be very scary and confusing. We won't be afraid, so let's create our Related news view.

At the top of the page, you will see **+ Add view**; by clicking on this, it will in fact allow us to create a new view. So, let's go ahead and do that now. We can see various fields on this page, but don't worry, we will go through each field now:

- **View name:** User-friendly name for our view. Drupal will create a machine name from this, which allows us to access when we try to alter it with code.
- **Description:** This description will appear on the **Views** admin page; it is more of a helper to other developers to explain what the view does.

- **View settings**:
    - **Show**: We can select what type of entity we want to show, depending on which we will change the options next to this field.
- **Tagged with**: This allows us to filter by tags on the Views admin page.
- **Sorted by**: We can order our content in views.
- **Page settings**: If we want to create our view with a page first, we can do that, and we can also add some basic settings for the page; click on the **Create a page** checkbox, and you will see a whole bunch of fields to enter.
- **Create a block**: We can add blocks to content, and views allows us to create these to display our content.

Understanding views

Now that we have set up our first view, let's get it to display some content.

We will create a latest news block, which will show our latest five news posts. By default, the view will display any content that is related to the content type, and it will only show the title. We will change this:

Fig 1.20: Views display page

In *Fig 1.20*, we can see there are three columns and in each column, there is an individual section. For now, we will just go through what we need for our **Latest news** block, but later we will go into more depth.

In views, we have **Displays**, these are the different ways that content is displayed. For the latest news and related news, we will, however, use the **Display** type of block. We will go into more detail later when we build our news listing page:

- **TITLE**: This is the title that will appear in our display.
- **FORMAT**: This is split into two sections:
    - **Format**: This is, by default, the type of layout, along with settings, for this format.
    - **Show**: This allows us to define how we want the content to be shown; we can either show based on a view mode or add fields to the view display.
- **FIELDS**: If we select the mentioned Format type to be fields, we will be able to add fields from our content type into this display. This allows us to customize our fields and how they are shown, and it ignores our view mode we created earlier.
- **FILTER CRITERIA**: We can set different filters that will depend on what content is to be shown. By default, **Published** is set to **Yes.**
- **SORT CRITERIA**: We can sort our content to display in many ways.

This is the first part we will cover. We want to create a very simple block that uses our default teaser view mode. To do this, we must click on the value next to **Show**; in this case, its **Fields**.

When we do this, a modal will appear with three radio buttons:

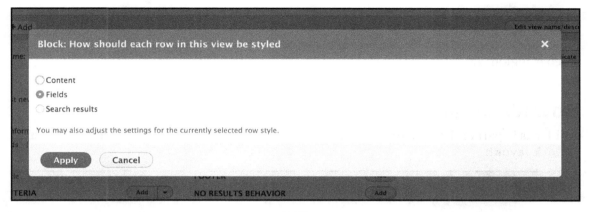

Fig 1.21

From *Fig 1.21*, we want to select **Content**. After we click on **Apply**, we will be shown a drop-down list that contains all the types of view modes we can have. We want to select the **Teaser** view mode.

When we apply this, we will see our news article along with its title, post information (author and timestamp of when it was created), and our **Read more** link in the preview. We see the post information because we had **Show submission information** checked inside the content type settings. Now that we have created our first view, let's place it on our sidebar.

Using blocks a brief overview

One of the cool things about Drupal is that we can control blocks of content from a UI. In our theme layout, we have the regions; these are what tells Drupal *Hey I'm a place for content, so let me show in the UI*. Regions allow us to place blocks of content inside it. We have various ways to create blocks.

In the previous versions of Drupal, we could only add block name, title, and content by default, this then had the ability to set certain settings on how it would display.

However, in Drupal 8, blocks are an entity type and with this come bundles. This means that we can now create custom block types and use the **Field UI** to add custom fields, and you guessed it, with that, we can organize our layout using **Manage display**; in Drupal 7, we had to use **Block Entities Are Nodes (BEAN)**--https://drupal.org/project/bean.

Block admin UI

Now we're excited about blocks; let's add our newly created **Latest news** block to our sidebar region.

How it's done

As blocks is part of the structure of Drupal, it's located under **Structure**. So, go to **Structure | Block layout**:

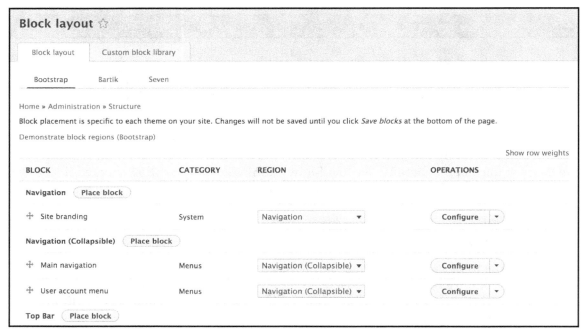

Fig 1.22: Block layout UI

As we can see in *Fig 1.22*, we have another table split up. This again allows us to drag our blocks to the region we want to show them in; this is the default setup for Drupal, with some default blocks.

The top part shows what themes are being used and each has its own setup for regions and blocks. We had set Bootstrap as our default theme, and so, its showing different regions from what the **Bartik** and **Seven** theme are showing. We will now add our block that we created in views. Once we have done this, we will explore how to create a different type of block.

Adding our block

In the previous versions of Drupal, we had a **Hidden** section; however, in Drupal 8, we have a cleaner and more usable approach--simply click on the region you want the block to be in--so for ours, we want to add our block to **Secondary**. If you move down to that title and click on **Place block**, a modal will appear that shows all our available blocks:

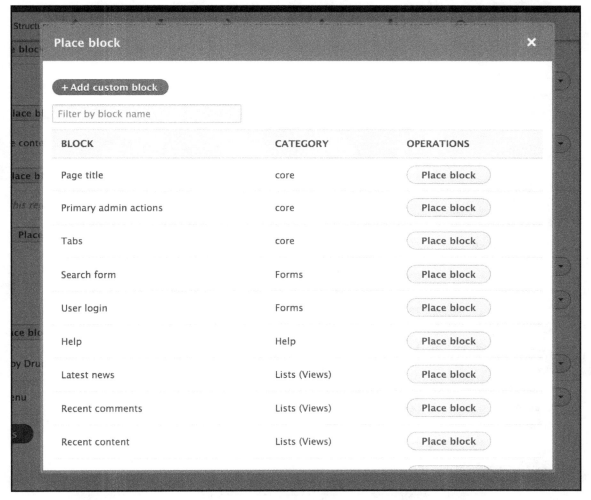

Fig 1.23: The Place block modal

Adding a block

Once this dialog appears, we will need to click **Place block** for it to be added to our regions, so let's find the block we created in views:

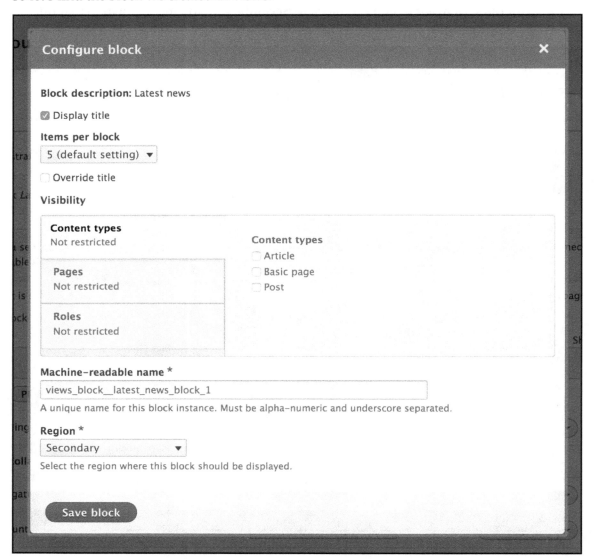

Fig 1.24: The Configure block modal

After selecting **Place block**, we are shown a new screen that lets us configure the settings for our block. As we created our block with views, we have a few more options than that of a standard block:

- **Display title**: This will show the title of the block created in views.
- **Items per block**: This allows us to override what number of items we set inside views.
- **Override title**: This allows us to override our title of the block. This will let us change the title we set in views; however, it won't change the title created in the view.
- **Visibility**: We can control where we want the block to show based on some certain requirements.
- **Content types**: We can restrict our block to show only on certain content types; for example, if we want it to just display on our **Post** content type, we will select this.
- **Pages**: We can set a list of pages we want to have shown or not shown here, and we can use wildcards as well to achieve this; for example, /node/*.
- **Roles**: We can restrict this block to specific user roles; however, we can also do this in our view. This is more useful with blocks not created in views.
- **Machine name**: We can set our machine name to be named however we like; this is so that we can access it in our theme or module, and it's also an identifier for us.
- **Region**: We can set which region we want our block to appear in.

Once happy with our configuration for our block, we can save it.

Now that we have saved and configured our block, we can view it in the block admin UI:

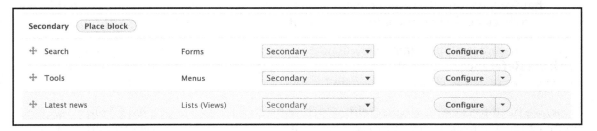

Fig 1.25

As is seen in the preceding screenshot, our block is at the bottom of the list in our **Secondary** region. We want to move it above search, so if you drag the row this block is in to the top so that it's above the **Search** block.

Great, so we have now added our block that we created in views to the top of sidebar 2, and it will show everywhere on the site.

Relating content

With any news website, there will always be related news articles that will draw the user to another article and then keep the user on the website for as long as possible.

What we will do

We want to create some more news posts, so let's create ten more and give different categories.

If you want to create a lot of dummy content, inside `devel` module (`https://drupal.org/project/devel`) is a submodule called `devel_generate`.

Great! Now we have created 10 extra news posts; we will now add a way to relate news posts.

Adding our entity reference field

Now that we have our 10 freshly created news posts, we want to relate them; to do this, we need to go back again to our content type. So, it's back to **Structure** | **Content types** | **Post**.

Once in our content type again, we will add our way to reference our related news posts. We have **Reference** in Drupal core, in Drupal 7 it was created using the contrib module `entity_reference`. However, we're in Drupal 8, and we have it in core!

Now, we need to click on **+ Add field**, which will again take us to our **Add field** page. Once on this page, we need to select **Reference** | **Content** from the **Add a new field** dropdown. Once we have done this, we will see our label field appear; let's add **Related posts** as our label.

Reference field category allows us to reference other entities and not just content!

After filling in our label, we will click on **Save and continue**, which takes us to our field configuration.

Moving on to the next part of field configuration, we are asked how many number of values can be shown within this field. We want to select unlimited; this is so that we don't limit the editor to how many posts are shown. Now we only want to show five, but we can amend this number later.

When we move on to the next page, we will see the settings for the field; as we are referencing content, we will select from content types **Post**. That's all you need to do to reference another piece of content. So now, we have added our content reference field.

The next step is to add five news articles to our main article; let's do that now. Returning to the content overview page /admin/content, we will edit our first piece of content created.

Edit content quickly by going to /node/{nid}/edit.

Once on the post we want to edit, move down to the **RELATED POSTS** part of the form:

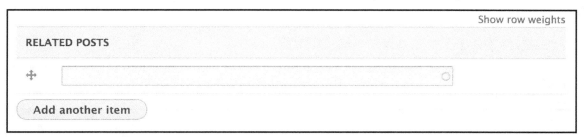

Fig 1.26: The Entity reference field

We can see that there's a text box with a grey circle to the right of it. This indicates to us, from a Drupal perspective, that it's an autocomplete field. So, if we now start to type a title from one of the posts we created, we will see the results it's found, and we can then select this article. You can see that it has our `Post title (nid)`; this allows us to easily see what the `nid` of the post is, but wait, we want to add another post that relates to this one.

Simply click on **Add another item**, and another field will appear. This means that we are now referencing two posts to this one. You'll also see that we have the crosshair to the left, which means that we can drag the rows up and down to change the weight, which in turn allows us to sort the order of the articles if, for example, we didn't want to order by date.

Once this is done, let's click on **Save and keep published.**

Great! Our post is updated!

We can now see our content with all our fields; it's not looking that pretty now though. Next, we will change this and use views again to display our related news articles.

How it works

Inside Drupal, every node has a nid and a uuid. When we reference this, the nid is added to the node object and is used as an ID to reference the other node to access the other node object. There is a relationship between our node and the other nodes as this is common with the type of database needed for Drupal.

Creating a related news block

We will use views again to create our related news block, so we need to go back into our previously created view--**Structure** | **Views**--and then select **Edit** for our latest news view:

Fig 1.27: Views display

In *Fig 1.27*, we can see that we have **Block*** and then **+ Add**; this is where we can see what displays are currently in our view:

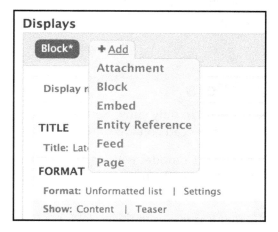

Fig 1.28: Add display type

If we click on **+ Add**, we will see a dropdown of **Display** types we can create. For this one, we want to create a block, so let's click on **Block**.

 If our display name has a * next to it, it means there are unsaved changes.

We will see that we now have **Block 2*** showing next to **Block.**

Now that we have created our new view display, it's time to explore our far column in our display.

In **Advanced**, we have the following sections:

- **Contextual filters**: These are arguments that will modify the output of our view; for example, if we only want to show content that our user has created, this allows us to reuse a view repeatedly without having to create multiple views for every user.
- **Relationships**: We can link our content type to other types of entity throughout Drupal. This then gives us access to that content and allows us to make what would be quite a large database join into something quick and simple.

- **Exposed form**: This allows us to use the filters we have created and make them into a user-based form in the style of a block, so we don't have to rely on it being just in our view; it can be below our views content.
- **Other**: This has various additional options to our view, but we won't be using these yet.

Using Contextual filters

For our related news block, we want to only show news based on the post's nid. Remember that we want to only show our referenced content for our post, and not any other posts.

If we click on **Add**, we will be shown a modal with various options to choose from; this modal is similar throughout the **Views** UI, and we can search for options that are similar to or an exact match.

We need to search for the ID that is our nid in this case. If we type nid, we get no results, unlike in the previous versions of Drupal where we would. As an entity has an **entity id**, we need to search for nid:

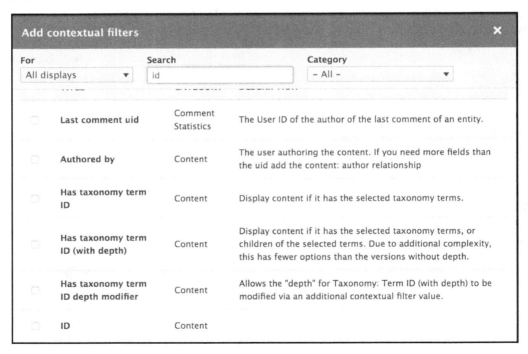

Fig 1.29: Results for ID

Great! We are getting some results, in fact, quite a few rely upon the term ID, so let's look for the exact match of just **ID** and select that. As we apply this and move to the next display, we can see a whole lot more of settings to choose from.

We want to choose **Provide default value**. Next, we are given a few more options to choose from. In this case, we want to take the ID from our URL, so select **Content ID from URL**. This allows us to even access the ID of our content either with a custom path set, because when we create our node, they are, by default, defined by `node/{nid}`, and we can access our `nid` from a custom path as this is stored in Drupal's routing system.

There are few more options here for us to choose from, which we will cover later.

Now that we have selected this option, we can apply these amends to our view.

Previewing content

In our view, we can see **Preview** if we move down the page, which is empty. This is because we are now reliant on a argument of the content ID. As we have nothing set, we have no argument to use. **Preview with contextual filters**. As our first content ID, we create 1. So, typing this into the field and clicking on the **Update** preview will hopefully show our content.

Oh wait, it shows our content for `node/1`; this is because we haven't set a relationship, so Drupal doesn't have anything to reference from. Let's fix this now.

Using relationships to show content

With our entity reference, we need to give our view the relationship so that we can access the referenced entity (node in our case).

We select **Add** under **Relationships**. In search of this modal for our case, we want to find our **Related posts** field, entity reference:

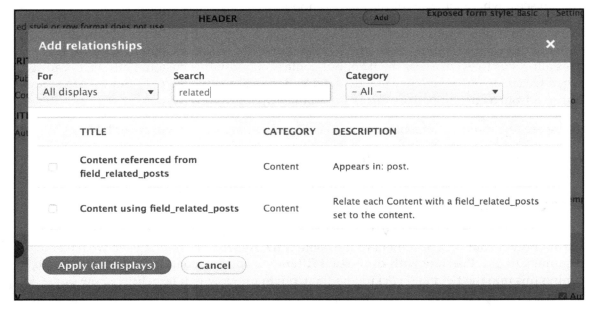

Fig 1.30: Relationships options

As you can see in *Fig 1.30*, we have searched for `related` and can see two rows with a similar looking field. The top row is just a direct relationship with **field_related_posts**, and the other one allows us to use the content relationships, so we can access content that we reference with that field anywhere in Drupal. So, we want to select **Content using field_related_posts**.

Getting back to the task in hand, select **This Block (override)** from the **For select** list, note how the **Apply** button changes to **Apply (this display)**.

We have (all displays) in the **Submit** button; this will change when we select from the top **For select** list at the top.

As we only want to show this relationship on this display, we need to select **This Block (override)** from the **For select** list; this changes our **Apply** button to **Apply (this display)**.

Now we can see our Related posts settings. As we don't want to change the format (in the left column of our **Views UI**), we select **Require this relationship** and then click on **Apply**.

Let's look at our preview. Okay, so it's still showing our node/1 content. This is because we still have our display to show a view mode for our content type. We can modify this to fields, but we want to keep it simple for now. To fix this, we need to tell our view, *Hey I want to use my relationship to display my content.*

So, going back to **Contextual Filters**, click on our **Content: ID**; we will see a new field called **Relationship.** Now, our view has nothing to go off, so we see our preview with the content of node/1. We need to change this so that our view knows that we want to show our referenced content in our node/1.

By changing it to the field we want to use our reference from, we will now tell our view to access this field's content that's referenced in the node we are on. We need to apply this, so we click on **Apply** and then, if we move down to our **Preview**, we will see the five related news posts we have referenced.

This is how we relate our content to our node. We currently have our view display named **Block 2**; this will mean nothing to us when we are working on it later. So, what we need to do is click on the text **Block 2** that is next to the **Display name** label, and a modal will appear with a field labelled **Administrative name**. We want to add a more descriptive name to this, so we shall call ours **Related news**; change **For** to **This block**, and we can click on the **Apply** button and then save the view.

Adding our new block to our Post content type

Now that we have created our **Related news** block, what we now need to do is to add this to appear on all **Post** content types.

Moving back to the **Block layout**, we will place our newly created **Related news** block below our main content. To do this, click on **Place block** and look for **Latest news: Related news**.

Note how the block is titled {VIEWNAME}: {Display name}.

So, once we click on **Place block**, we will see another page that has given us more options; we can see an open tab called **Content types**, along with some checkboxes with our content types listed next to them. As we only want our **Related news** to appear on the **Post** content type, we click on **Save** and that's it, our block will now show on all **Post** content types.

Oh wait, our block is listed above our **Content** block, which means that, yeah you guessed it, our **Related news** block will be displayed above our **Main page content**. We don't really want this to happen, so let's move this block below our **Main page content** block. Yeah, that's better! Now, we need to click on **Save blocks** to save these amends and then we can visit node/1 to see our **Related news** block.

Now that we have our five **Related news** items showing, let's tidy up the display of the **Post** content type view mode.

Making our display look better

Next, we want to make the display of our content look better than it currently is; we will do this all inside the **Form** UI. Let's get back to the **Manage display** page on our content type and tidy up what we have. Go to the content types **Manage display** section, or by quickly navigating to /admin/structure/types/manage/post/display.

Looking at this page, we are working with the fields set inside our content type; let's move the following into **Disabled**:

- **Links**
- **Post category**
- **Related posts**

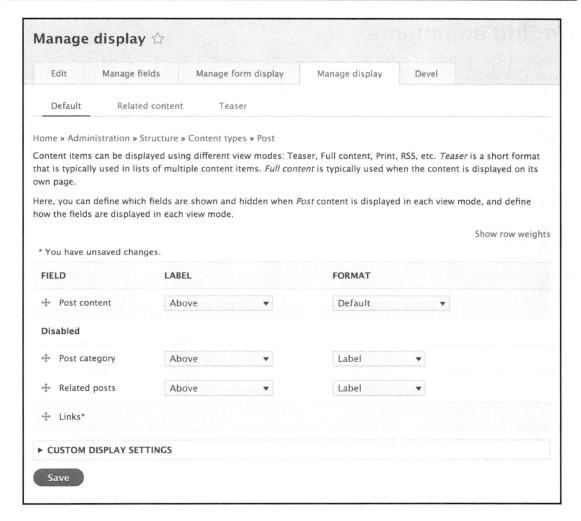

Fig 1.31: Content type manage display

In *Fig 1.31*, we have moved these fields into **Disabled**. Once we save this, the changes will appear on our **Post** content, and if we return to our **Post**, we can see the following:

- Post details (author and time)
- Main content
- Related news blocks

That's all we need for now; we will make this look better later.

Adding comments

Interaction with your user is key to any website; it keeps the user on your website for longer. One of the great ways to do this is to allow users to comment on the posts. This can also help with showing that you're open about what you write and is a great way to communicate with your audience and for them to communicate with you.

Drupal has a core module called **comments**, which does exactly this. It allows your posts to have comments made by your users, it's as simple as that.

How do comments work

As everything is an entity in Drupal, you guessed it, comments are an entity type to! In Drupal 8, we can have multiple types of comment; this also links nicely into the way comments can be moderated. However, moderating comments can be hardwork, and can be regularly targeted by spam bots. There are, however, other solutions that can link to this; Disqus (`https://disqus.com`) being one of them, and yes, there is a `contrib` module for that (`https://drupal.org/project/disqus`); briefly, what this does is to create a field, which means you can attach Disqus comments too.

However, for our Posts, we want to keep it with Drupal core's approach.

Comment types

As per any entity type, we can add bundles. Comment is an entity type; the fact that we can have different comment types for different content is great!

It also uses **Field** UI and therefore we have the same abilities as the content types view modes that we explored earlier in the chapter.

What this means for us

As comment is an entity type and utilizes the **Field** UI, it means that we can now add fields to our comments, which gives us the ability to add a 5-star rating widget or a file upload. For our website, however, we will keep it simple and allow for just a message field.

Now, let's see the comment types and where to modify them from. It's in **Structure**, so let's click on **Structure**. We will see comment types in the page listing; if we click on that, we get redirected to another page--it looks like our content type listings page:

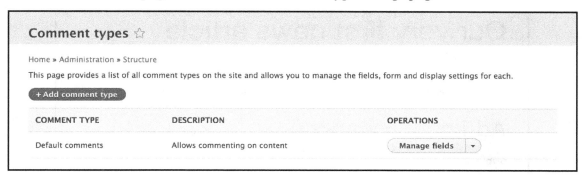

Fig 1.32: Comment type listings

If we are to look at the comment types as per *Fig 1.32*, we already have a comment type of **Default comments**. If we click on **Manage** fields, we are taken to our field listing page, which shows a **Comment** field, which is just a text area.

Attaching comments

As we want our visitors to be able to comment on the posts on the website, we now need to add our comment field to our **Post** content type.

To do this, we need to go back to our Post content type and to **Manage fields**. Let's add out comment field into our content type. Remember that we covered it earlier in the chapter, and click on **+ Add field.**

After doing this again, we will be shown a dropdown to select **Comments** from under **General** in the list. After adding this, we are shown a **Comment type** dropdown. If we were to add another comment type, we would see all the types listed here. However, as we only have our default one, we will just see **Default comments**; now from here, click on **Save field settings**.

With any field type, there are specific field settings. As we want to keep our comments to function the same as other comments from websites, we will leave all the settings to be the same, but we can disable comments at a later stage, change the amount shown by default, and amend how and where the reply comment form will appear.

Right now, to see our comments field in action, if we return to our first news post, which is at /node/1, we can see our comments field that has generated a subject field and comment field:

Fig 1.33: Rendered comments field

Moderation

With any website that allows user input into forms, we need to control how this is managed as we will likely get targeted by our spam bots, which tend to create a new account and then target the comments fields. So, we need to be able to manage our comments.

Fortunately, this has already been thought of, and we have a comment management page that allows us to moderate and manage the comments posted on the website. There is a permission that allows this to be skipped, so this can just be set for content editors/moderators of the posts.

 Logged in as user ID (uid) 1, we have access to all permissions; it's just a default functionality in Drupal.

With the moderation page, this allows us to quickly approve/decline comments that have been made.

However, if as stated earlier, we have our superadmin (user id 1) or our permission of **Skip comment** approval, then we will have the comments posted without moderation.

If we create an incognito window in our browser, we can test how a user will see the comments. Once we are back on our website, go to /user/register and enter details to create a new user:

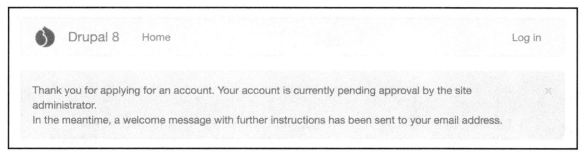

Fig 1.34: User creation message

In *Fig 1.34*, we can see our message showing that the user has been created. As we have it set so that every user registration must be approved, we need to go back to our other browser window and accept the user.

If we click on **People**, it will then take us to the **User Management** page. On this page, we can manage various aspects for our users.

These include the following:

- Creating users
- Editing users
- Adding/removing roles from users
- Blocking users

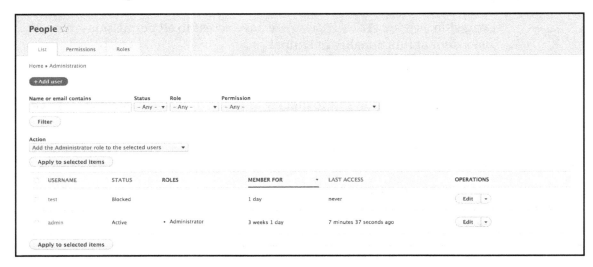

Fig 1.35: People administration page

In *Fig 1.35*, we can see that there are three tabs at the top of the page:

- **List**: This page shows the users we have on our Drupal site; we're currently on this page
- **Permissions**: This allows us to add/remove permissions from user roles
- **Roles**: This is where we can give a user privileges by assigning them permissions as a group on the permissions page

Before we move to permissions, let's approve this user. Next to our username, there's a checkbox; if we check this and then under the **Action select** list at the top of the table, we can see **Unblock the selected user(s)** in the list, clicking **Apply to selected items** will do that, and it also means that we can apply this action to multiple user accounts, so there is no need to go through each individual account.

This means that we can now login. Keeping the administrator to approve the user is great; however, it can require a lot of management and depending on the number of visitors you have to your site, this can be very time consuming.

Permissions

We briefly covered what permissions were earlier; in our case, we want to set a permission to our user role of **Authenticated user**.

If we click on **Permissions**, we will be taken to a page showing all our permissions and which roles have these permissions.

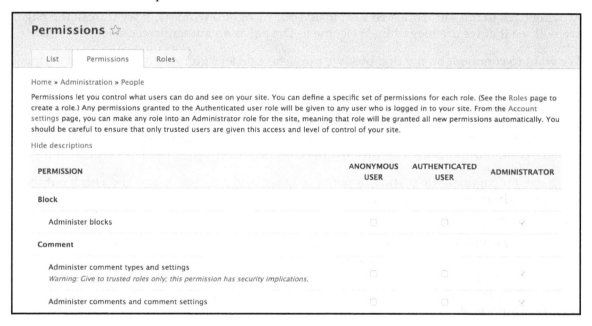

Fig 1.36: The Permissions administration page

In *Fig 1.36*, we can see that our permissions page is split into four main columns; the columns increase as we add more user roles. When we create a new permission inside our module's `routing.yml` file (which we will cover later); this is displayed in the left column, and will allow us to assign our new permission to our user role.

Administrator role has access to all permissions by default.

We want to turn off our **Skip comment approval** permission for our **Authenticated user.** Simply uncheck the checkbox that is listed in the row that our role name is listed in at the top of the table. Once this is done, scroll down and click on **Save permissions.**

Great! We have just changed our first permission! Feel the awesome power of permissions now!

Moving back to our authenticated user inside our incognito window, if we refresh the page, we will see that we are logged in. Welcome to Drupal as an authenticated user!

We want to comment on the first post we published, so let's go back to node/1 and do this there.

Add a comment and click on **Save**; upon doing this, we see a message at the top saying **Your comment has been queued for review by site administrators and will be published after approval**. This is exactly what we want to see; remember our permission we changed earlier? Well, this has caused us to allow the comment to be approved before publishing.

We have our comment field and our permission set, and now we can go and check out the comment administration page. Remember that comments are listed inside /admin/content/comment.

As we can see, there is **Unapproved comments (1)**, which is exactly what we're expecting to see as we haven't approved this comment yet. To approve and publish this comment, we just click on the **Unapproved comments (1)** tab, and we will see our new comment that has been created. To allow and publish this comment, we can see a similar interface to the content administration.

With any comment, we can approve, decline, edit, or delete it. Now, let's approve this comment; if we check the checkbox next to the comment, and then under **Update options**, we select the select list with **Publish the selected comments** and click on **Update**, our comment will be published on our website.

Moving back to our incognito window, if we refresh the page, we will see our comment showing up following our news article.

If, however, we look at our sidebar, we can see **Add comment** showing up, so as a refresher, what we want to do is to create a new view mode for our **Post** content type called **Teaser listing**.

If you get stuck doing this, refer to the part where we go through creating our view mode earlier on in the chapter.

Welcome back if you had to refresh your memory, if you didn't, great! Go have a well-deserved cup of tea (I am from England, after all).

As we now have our new view mode created and assigned to our content type and our Manage display, we can modify the fields we don't want to show. We don't want our comments to show up now, we just want our links to be there for now as we will soon be modifying how it looks within our theme! However, before we get excited about moving into working with our theme, let's go ahead and create a listing and filter page to show our posts.

Listing and filtering content

We have already touched on views and how powerful it is, but let's go even deeper as we're just touching the surface of it with how powerful it is.

So, getting back to views `/admin/structure/views`, let's go into the view we were working on earlier. Once we're back in our view, let's add a new display and this time, select **Page**. You will see that the layout is slightly different than that of the block display. As we are creating a page, we need to set a path; otherwise, there is no way for us to access the page. Let's add our path of `/news`; once this is done, we want to add two filters--date and category--this will allow us to filter our content by certain criteria.

Exposed filters

Inside views, we can have two approaches for filter; first are filters predefined, so by default, we have **Publishing status: Yes**, which is set to show only published content.

We then have our exposed filters, which allows the filter we set to be shown to the user; it will create a form and by default, it appears above the view content. If you want to, you can move the exposed filters below your content, or you can move them to another region entirely if you're feeling adventurous!

Getting back to creating our exposed filter, we need to add our category type; so, clicking on **Add** next to the **Filters** title will make a modal show up, which is like the modals we saw earlier.

Start by searching for **category** inside our **Search** text field. Again, you will see the fields filter down; in this case, we have one result. Select the field row by checking the checkbox.

Remember to change the **For** dropdown at the top, otherwise it will affect all our view displays, which will modify every other view display.

Great! So, we have now added our **category** field, and it will only show for this view display; we can now expose our category filter, so let's go ahead and do this:

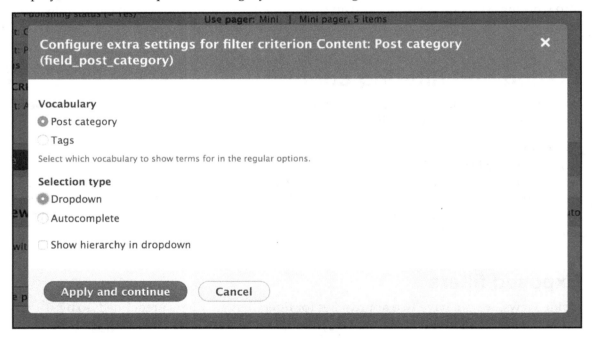

Fig 1.37: Exposed filter modal

In *Fig 1.37*, we can see our settings for this filter item; it's listing the taxonomy vocabularies we have. We want to select **Post category**, then dropdown, and after that, select **Show hierarchy in dropdown**, and click on **Apply and continue**; we will then be shown another page with a lot more settings:

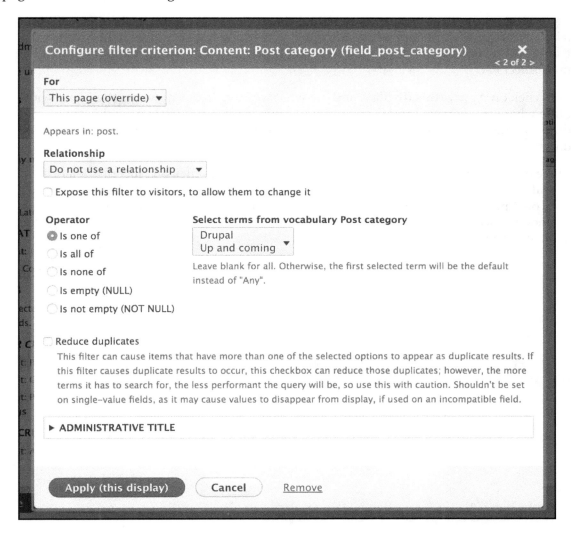

Fig 1.38: Filter settings

So from *Fig 1.38*, we can see that there are more settings, **Operator** and **Select terms from vocabulary Post category** are straightforward. We can restrict our page to only show certain posts that have certain terms. However, we want to allow the user to do this themselves, so let's go ahead and check **Expose this filter to visitors, to allow them to change it**.

As soon as we do this, we have more settings to configure. We want to change the filter label to **Categories** and then we want to keep everything else the same. If, however, we want to allow multiple selections for a category, then this will change the filter output to a multiselect list.

Let's click on **Apply (this display)** and see what we have in our preview. Well, that's not quite what we want; we can see our exposed filter and our results, but we're seeing duplicate results. To fix this, we need to aggregate our results so that we only see our node once and not duplicated.

Move over to the right column and under **Use aggregation**, click on **No**; once again, a modal will appear. In this case, as we want to aggregate our results, check **Aggregate** and click on **Apply (this display).** Now, let's check our preview. Great! We are only showing our nodes once. Now that we have created our first listing page for our nodes, let's go look at it; click on **Save** and then go to /news:

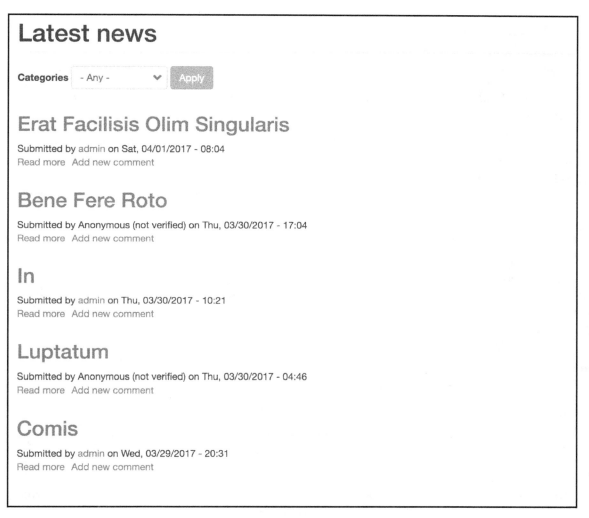

Fig 1.39: The news listing page

As we can see in *Fig 1.39*, this is our newly created news listing page. By default, it shows all news articles, in order of the most recent.

Restricting content by role

We now have our news showing up to any user, but what if we want to restrict news to just authenticated users, to give them an incentive to sign up to the website and view members-only content.

How to do it

To restrict content to certain user roles, we need to install a contrib module called **content access** (`https://drupal.org/project/content_acess`).

Once downloaded, enable the module. Remember to **clear your cache** and then go to the **Content type** page if you want to create a new content type.

This content type will be called **Restricted post**; once we save this, we will then see a new tab called **Access control**; this is where we find the configuration for how the node is displayed and for which role:

ROLE BASED ACCESS CONTROL SETTINGS

View any restricted_post content	View own restricted_post content	Edit any restricted_post content	Edit own restricted_post content
☑ Anonymous user	☑ Anonymous user	☐ Anonymous user	☐ Anonymous user
☑ Authenticated user	☑ Authenticated user	☐ Authenticated user	☐ Authenticated user
☐ Administrator	☐ Administrator	☑ Administrator	☑ Administrator

Delete any restricted_post content	Delete own restricted_post content	
☐ Anonymous user	☐ Anonymous user	Note that users need at least the *access content* permission to be able to deal in any way with content. Furthermore note that content which is not published is treated in a different way by drupal: It can be viewed only by its author or users with the *administer nodes* permission.
☐ Authenticated user	☐ Authenticated user	
☑ Administrator	☑ Administrator	

Fig 1.40: Content access for restricted post

In *Fig 1.40*, we can see that there are various grouped checkboxes that show what user role can access the content. For this content type, we want to uncheck all **Anonymous user** roles; this is because we only want the **Authenticated user** and any role above that to be able to access this content.

From here, we can now go and create some restricted posts. We will then show the restricted posts inside the news listing and latest news block; however, the **Anonymous users** will not be able to see this, they will be shown an **Access Denied** page; this is what we want to achieve.

Let's go and create some content that only our authenticated users can see. Referring to earlier, we need to go to **Manage | Content** and once on that page, we need to click on + **Add content**.

We can see our **Post** content type and our **Restricted post** content type. As we want to create our first restricted post, let's click on the **Restricted post**.

Now we can enter our restricted post content; this page will look familiar to earlier, when we created our Posts. Once this post is created, we will only be able to see this as an authenticated user.

Adding restricted content to views

Moving back to the view we created earlier, we need to allow the restricted news items to show in our listings. This is a really simple process, and Drupal does the heavy lifting for us in terms of restricting the content to the user roles that are meant to see them.

Once we are inside the view, we need to add the content type to our displays. As we don't have any fields that reference other nodes inside our restricted news content type, there will be no restricted news content to show inside the **Related post** view display.

If we add our Restricted post content type to the view, restricted posts will appear in these views. To do this, we move down to **Filter criteria** and click on **Content type**; this will launch a modal that will already have our **Post** content type checked. To add our restricted post content type to our view, we need to check **Restricted post** and click on **Apply (All displays)**.

As our restricted posts do not have an entity reference to any other posts, we won't see any of our restricted posts in this view, which will also mean that because we have no content that meets this criterion, we won't even have the block display. However, if we remember that when we added our **Related news** block to our **Post** content type, we only selected it to show on **Post** content type, so we don't have to worry about this showing.

If we move back to our site, as a logged in user, we will see that our **Restricted post** content will show up. However, if we move over to our anonymous user, we can only see our normal posts. This is because the settings we applied to our **Restricted post** content type are working, and so are our view displays; they are working hand in hand with the Drupal access system.

Editing content

In Drupal 8, we no longer need to download, install, and configure our WYSIWYG editor. It comes in Drupal core!

When adding or editing content, we have a field that has a filtered content selected, and we will see the WYSIWYG editor. By default, we have three formats available to us:

- **Basic HTML.**
- **Restricted HTML.**
- **Full HTML.**
  - We also have **Plain text**, which does not show an editor. With formats, we can set certain rules that will limit what the user with that role can do. This varies from image uploads to HTML markup.

To modify this configuration, go to **Configuration**; this page is where much of the configuration for our core, `contrib`, and custom modules is located. To the left-hand side, we have the **Content authoring** section with **Text formats and editors**. Once we are on the **Text formats and editors** page, we will see a list of format types:

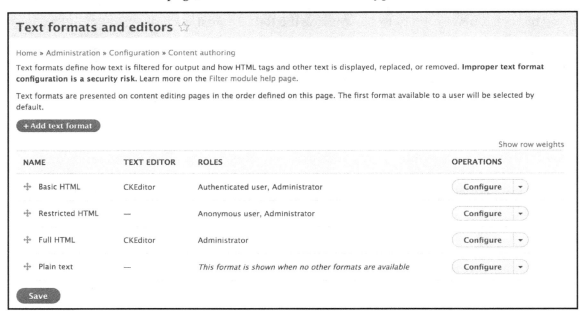

Fig 1.41: Text formats and editors configuration

- **Name**: Our user-friendly name for the type of format
- **Text editor**: Allows us to select which editor is used; by default, the editor is **CKEditor**
- **Roles**: The filter can be assigned to specific roles to allow one role more control than another
- **Operations**: Allows us to control the format

Let's go through the configuration for a text filter, if we click on **Configure** in the **Full HTML** format, we'll see what control we have for the format.

On this page, we can see that roles and text editor can be assigned; moving down, there is a toolbar with buttons that can be moved into the active toolbar, which will be shown to that user role when the text format is selected. The rest of the page allows us to set the filtering for the editor itself, to keep it clean and not pose a potential security risk to our site.

Moving to the frontend

In Drupal 8, we have moved to a new frontend layer system called **Twig**, which is the theming layer component used in Symfony 2.

Twig allows non-PHP developers to work on the frontend of the site, as it has its own syntax--`{{ variable }}`.

This not only looks cleaner, but also makes it easier to convert a static HTML template into a Drupal theme. There is a lot more control for us, as developers, to work with the frontend layer and no longer will we rely on classes on the frontend to style pages. We have the ability of using libraries to add a library to a global aspect of the site or individual pages and content types.

Earlier on, in **Getting started**, we went through the basics of what is in a theme. We now want to make use of the libraries, which allows us to define our CSS/JavaScript and use it in our templates. One of the really great things about this is with websites using a lot of nonstandard fonts and third-party services, such as Google fonts; we can allow this to be added into our theme layer in a very simple approach. Let's add **Khula** to our theme.

Adding CSS and JavaScript

As our theme is called blueprints, we need to create our libraries `yml` file. We need to reference the library name inside our theme info file.

Inside `blueprint.info.yml`, we add the following:

- `blueprint.info.yml`

  ```
  # Libraries
   libraries:
    - blueprint/global
    - blueprint/fonts
  ```

- `blueprint.libraries.yml`

  ```
  # Libraries
  global:
    version: 1.x
    css:
     theme:
        css/style.css: {}
    js:
       js/javascript-file.js: {}
  fonts:
    css:
    theme:
      '//fonts.googleapis.com/css?family=Khula:regular,bold': {
  type: external, minified: true }
  ```

What the preceding code snippet does is that it defines our library name and then allows us to add CSS and JavaScript to our theme.

By creating our `style.css` file and declaring our new font name, we will see that when we cache rebuild `drupal cache:rebuild`, it will now show our site with the Khula font being used:

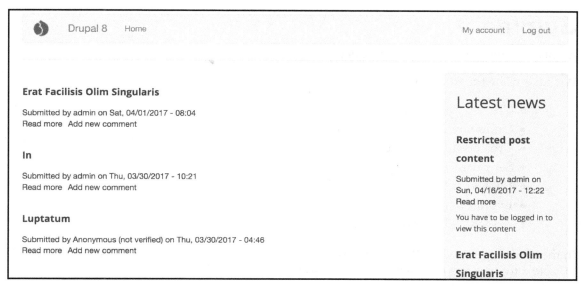

Fig 1.42: After applying our new CSS library

As in *Fig 1.42*, we can see that our Khula font has applied to the site. After performing a cache rebuild again, it shows on the page.

If we want to add inside a specific template, we just need to add this to our template files. In the previous versions of Drupal, we would use `drupal_add_js()` or `drupal_add_css()`. This has now been replaced with `{{ attach_library('themename/library-name); }}`.

 Drupal 8 now uses asset libraries for CSS and JS. Before this change, in order to add asset libraries in a theme, the library would have to be added site-wide or a theme would need to implement a preprocess function (which requires writing PHP)--`https://www.drupal.org/node/2456753`.

Further on in the book, we will go into more detail about theming. This will go into detail about using our libraries, variables, conditions, and how to debug the templates.

Summary

In this chapter we have started to uncover the power of Drupal core.

We have done the following:

- Created and understood what a content type is
- Understood how fields and display modes work
- Created different types of fields
- Set permissions for fields
- Looked at the block plugin and how we can control them
- Explored how views works and why we use it
- Added a library to our theme

In the next chapter we will look at how to make a fundraising website, in this chapter we will start to look at a the user system and some custom module development.

3
Get Fundraising with Drupal

Fundraising websites such as JustGiving, Virgin Money, and GoFundMe are
an effective way to do something great and support charities to make a difference to
someone's life.

In this chapter, we will create a fundraising website where a fundraising page can be
created by someone explaining what they are doing, who they are fundraising for, and
when. This will then allow someone else to "donate" an amount to support it.

Now we know a lot of site building techniques and have an understanding of how to create
content types, fields, views, users, and blocks we will cover less of how to build things that
we have previously covered, but will explain more about the new things we will cover.

We will cover the following in this chapter:

- Creating a content type called donation
- Creating a content type called fundraising page
- Allowing users to sign up and donate
- Creating a dashboard for the fundraiser
- Introducing our first custom module
- Creating a donation form using Form API

What will we learn?

We will learn how to allow certain roles to create content from what we have learned
previously, and then move on to cover how to allow these users to edit their own content,
showing a dashboard of all their fundraising content. We will also cover allowing
authenticated users to submit a donation; we won't integrate a payment gateway for this as
there are so many we can pick from.

The donation will then appear on the fundraising page and an email notification will be sent out to the pledger. After this, we will explore how to make our module work with twig templates.

Getting started

We need to duplicate the site that we previously made and change the settings and configuration in our local environment.

Once this is done, we can do `drush si standard -y`; this will give us a clean installation of Drupal. Once we have done this, we need to enable our custom theme, as earlier.

Creating our fundraising pages

Our fundraising page will be split into two parts: the first part will be the actual fundraising information, and the second part will be the donations submitted on the fundraising page.

The way we will do this is that the logged in user will be able to create a fundraising page; this will use a reference to a new content type called donation. We can also create a new entity type for this entirely, but we will keep it simple by creating a content type.

So, to move on with this, let's create our donation content type. We want to keep this simple, so we need two fields for this, as the author is saved upon being created.

Donation content type

When a user who is logged in visits a fundraising page, they have the option to donate. For this, we just need two fields: one called `Donation amount`, which is a `Number > float` field type, and the other just a name, in case they want to change their name on the donation.

Fundraising content type

We will add a way the donation is linked to the fundraising page. This will be done via entity reference and will store the amount donated, name, and the user who created it. This is how we know the amount that has been donated, and we can then take all the referenced donations and add them up and calculate how much is remaining.

To do this, we need to create our fundraising content type; we want it to allow display of the fundraising page, on which we will show a description of the pledge. Along with this, we want to set an amount we want to achieve, and the date we want to achieve it by. We can add to this later if we want.

Now, add the following fields:

- **Fundraising description**: This will be `Text` (formatted, a long with summary).
- **Fundraising amount**: This will be a `Number>float` field type.
- **Date to achieve by**: This will be a date field.
- **Fundraising state**: This will be a `List` (integer) that will allow for an open or closed state. In the field settings for this, add `Open` into the text area, and beneath that, add `Closed`. When we go to the next step, Drupal will create a number to assign to the value, which will be the key that we will use.
- **Donations**: This will be an entity reference to our donation content type. Upon creating the fundraising page, there will be donations.

Now we want to allow anonymous users to create an account and log in and start a pledge. Next, we will look at user account settings.

Registering users

With Drupal, we have our core ability for users to register and create accounts. We can also control what the user must fill out to register.

For this, we will explore how user registration works and what we can control from Drupal UI.

Account settings

We control the account configuration inside **Configuration** | **Account settings**:

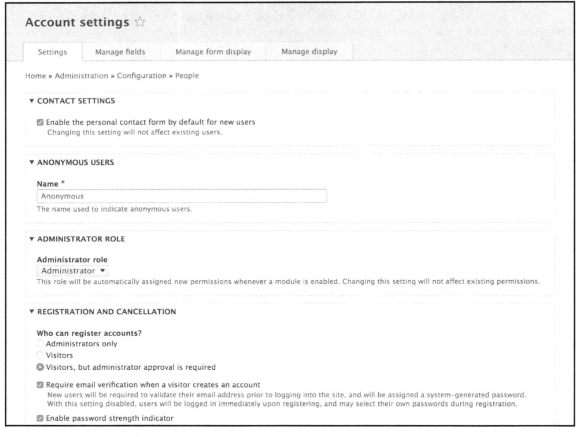

Fig 1.0: Account settings

This section is split up into four tabs, which looks very similar to our content types layout:

- **Settings**: This allows us to set specific settings, authentication, and define notifications sent out upon certain actions
- **Manage fields**: This allows us to add fields, and also reuse fields from elsewhere in Drupal

- **Manage form display**: This allows us to amend how the form is shown to the users registering
- **Manage display**: This allows us to amend how the profile page is shown to the user

Starting on the **Settings** page, we can see that the page is split into multiple sections, as per *Fig 1.0*:

- **CONTACT SETTINGS**: If we want to allow users to be able to contact each other
- **ANONYMOUS USERS**: By default, Anonymous is what is used to describe our anonymous users; this can be changed to anything you like
- **ADMINISTRATOR ROLE**: This allows an admin role to be set; by default, it's set to Administrator, but it can be assigned to another user role and therefore will give that role the same permissions as administrators
- **REGISTRATION AND CANCELLATION**: There are various settings here that control how the registration works
- **Notification email address**: When a system mail is sent out in relation to a user

Creating our users

Firstly, we need to create our new user roles, so as before, if we go to **People** from the admin menu, we will be shown our people admin interface. From here, we can select roles.

For this website, we just need the default roles:

- **Authenticated**: This will be our default user role, which can create fundraising content and donate

We want to allow our Authenticated role the ability to create fundraising pages that only they and an administrator can edit. We don't want a user to be able to delete a fundraiser page; if they want to do this, they must email the administrator. We also want them to be able to donate, but we don't want them to be able to edit or delete donations.

We want to give our **Authenticated users** the ability to create and edit **fundraising** pages and create **Donation** pages.

Authenticated users

- **Fundraising page:** Create new content
- **Fundraising page:** Edit own content
- **Donation:** Create new content

Building the fundraising page

As we have now created our user roles, we can begin to create our first **fundraising** page. Let's create our user, and from there, we will create our first **fundraising** page:

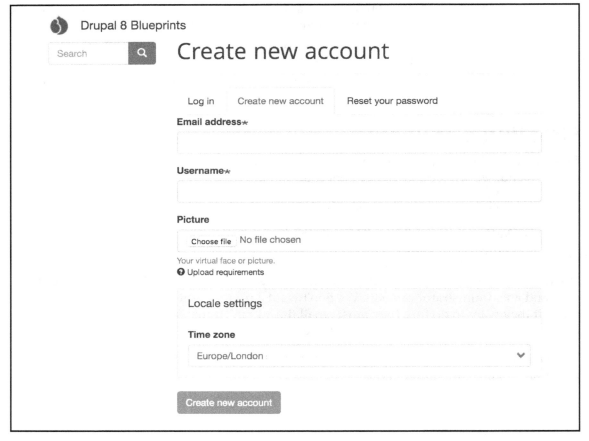

Fig 1.1: Registration page without the password fields

Open an incognito window in Chrome, and then get to the registration page; what you will notice is that there is nowhere to enter a password. For this registration form, we want to allow our users to add a password and then immediately be logged in. To do this, we need to go back to our **Account settings** page and scroll down to **Registration and cancellation**.

First, we need to change who can register for an account. We need to change this from **Visitors**, but administrator approval is required for **Visitors**.

Directly beneath this, we can see `Require email verification when a visitor creates an account`; this is currently checked, so we now need to uncheck it. This will now show two password fields on our registration field, along with the default Drupal password strength indicator. Once you have done this, return to the incognito window and you will see that we have two password fields and a password strength indicator.

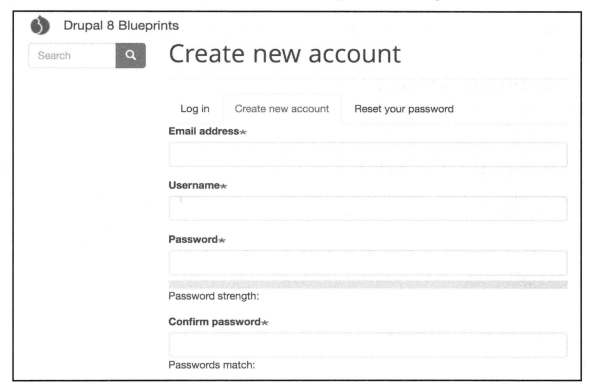

Fig 1.2: Create new account with password.

Once we fill out this form, we will be redirected to the home page of the site, and we will see a notification saying **Registration successful. You are now logged in.**

In fact, all we can see is basic navigation, and within that, we will now see **My account** and **Logout.** There is also a navigation menu in the left sidebar. This is how our users can add content; we can make this look nicer if we want later.

If we now click on **Add content**, we will be taken to our **Add content** page; on this page, we will see our two types of content that can be created.

Now go and click on the **fundraising** page. What we will see is the form from the fields we created earlier. Let's fill this out so that we can see our **fundraising** page in action; we want to fill out everything apart from donations, and we can hide this later using **Manage form display**.

We have now successfully created our first **fundraising page**, well done!

Creating a dashboard

As we have created our basic donation page, we want to create a page that will show all the current pages set up for fundraisers.

Going back to views, we will create a view that uses a page display and shows our **fundraising** pages only created by the current logged in user.

So, we will create a new view called `Fundraiser dashboard` and select the type of content. Following this, we want to check **Create a page**:

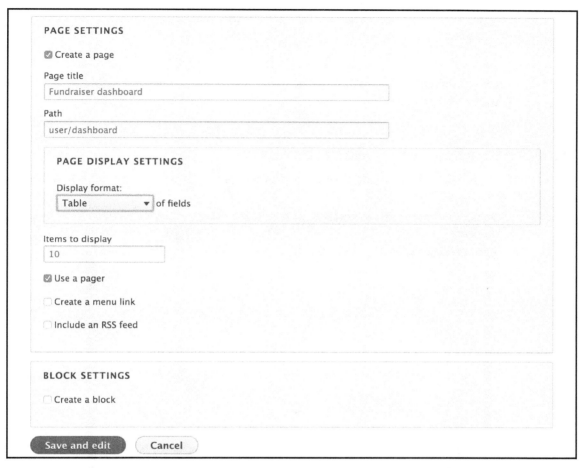

Fig 1.3: View display settings

Now, as in *Fig 1.3*, we will change our path to /user/dashboard and then change **Page display settings** and **Display format** to **Table**. Now, click on **Save and edit**.

We want to add the following fields to our view:

- Created date
- View node
- Edit node

As previously, let's click on **Add** in the **Fields** section; this will bring up our modal window. From here, let's select:

- **Authored on**
- **Link to content**
- **Link to edit content**

Understanding view field settings

Each field in a view has multiple field settings that we can utilize. Let's take a look at the **Authored on** field settings:

Fig 1.4: Field settings in a view

As we can see in *Fig 1.4*, there are multiple parts to our field settings:

- **Create a label**: This allows us to have a label next to the field content; we can leave it to show the default label text, or we can change it.

- **Place a colon after a label**: With our label we just set, we can add a simple colon next to our label; this is to allow us to show our fields and distinguish them between our label and field content.

- **Formatter**: With the fields, we can have multiple formatter types based on the type of field they are; in this example, we have a default option that will just display our date, or we can choose a time option that will just show how long ago the post was created. If we change the option of our formatter, we get a reloaded form that gives us different options.

- **STYLE SETTINGS**: We can control how our field label, content, and outer wrappers are created and what type of HTML is used for the label or field; this allows us to use HTML elements, and we can even add custom classes to these elements to give us more control over how we style our items. By default, however, the field will have default classes added to the `views-field views-field-{fieldname}` field.

- **REWRITE RESULTS**: We again have more settings to modify how our output for the field is displayed.

- **Override the output of this field with custom text**: This allows us to change how the field output is displayed and ignores all previous style settings. It's handy if you want to add some custom elements to your content that you couldn't do in the preceding settings. However, as we have Ttwig, we can also use Twig templates to create these output adjustments.

- **Output this field with a custom link**: We can change the link URL using replacement patterns; this allows us to amend the attributes inside our link. Again, this gives us more control and lets us use tokens to do this.

- **Trim this field to a maximum number of characters**: This is handy when we have an article that we want to show a limited number of characters, and is used more for blurbs of content.

- **Trim only on a word boundary**: This allows us to trim our content at the end of a word, which will affect the number of characters, as it will stop at the end of the next word in the value.

- **Add "..." at the end of trimmed text**: This allows us to show our user that there is more to this content, and usually, this is followed by a **Read more** link, which will take our user to the full content. The next four options allow us to tidy up our value and remove any unwanted HTML or white spaces. However, we do have the option to keep HTML within this value.

- **NO RESULTS BEHAVIOUR**: If we have no value for this field, we can display some replacement text or hide the output.
- **ADMINISTRATIVE TITLE**: This helps us see what the field is instead of displaying the default field title and field name.

Now that we have seen the great configuration settings for our fields, let's go and just save the default settings for this field as we can come back later and change these if we want to.

Showing user's their content

We only want our logged in user's to see the content they have created; in this case, we just want them to see their **fundraising** pages created.

To do this, we need to go to the right and click on **Advanced** and then **Contextual filters**, and click on the **Add** button; as earlier, this will then bring up a modal with a lot of options to choose from. In this case, we want to select **Configure contextual filter: Content: Authored by** and then **Provide default value**, and change **Type** to **User ID from logged in user** and then click on **Apply.** This will then change our **Preview**. To view the content that we have for this user in the contextual filter text field, we need to put 2, as this is the UID of the user that created this **fundraising** page.

We won't, however, need to do this later, as it takes the argument based on our logged in user's user ID.

Now that we have created our dashboard view, we will move on to creating our form that will appear on the page.

Allowing users to donate

In this section, we will explore how to create a form that will allow users to be able to donate. We will call this module **Donate**.

What we will do

We will be starting to write our very first custom module!

How modules work

In Drupal, we have our core set of modules; we also have contrib modules that are available at `https://drupal.org`. Modules allow us to extend Drupal, and sometimes we need to make our own custom modules.

Structure of a module

Inside a module, we have a few files that are needed, but to tell Drupal about our new module, we just need one file--`MYMODULE.info.yml`. This is what tells Drupal our module details; we only need this for us to enable our custom module.

Creating our module

Now, let's create our module. We will place this inside `/modules` and then create a directory called `custom`; inside this directory, we will create a directory for our module to go into. This should be named the same as what we will name our module files.

donate.info.yml

We need to create an `.info.yml` file to tell Drupal about our module. This is required for all modules.

```
name: Donation form
description: Allows logged in users to donate
core: 8.x
type: module
package: Donate
```

- **Name**: This is the name of our module and how it will appear inside our module listing page.
- **Description**: This is used as a quick view of what the module does; it should be short but precise.
- **Core**: This tells Drupal that this module is for any release of Drupal 8.
- **Type**: This is how Drupal knows what it is; we can have a module or theme.
- **Package**: This is how we group our modules.

As with any amendment in Drupal, we need to do a cache rebuild, so run `drupal cache:rebuild`.

Once this is done, we will need to go into our modules list inside Drupal, so go to **Extend** and look for the section name called **DONATE**:

Fig 1.5: Our new Donate module

Now that we have done this, we can start adding to our module. For our form, we need to create a form. We have a structured approach that we follow, which uses `PSR-4` namespaces. This allows us to autoload our files in Symfony.

Throughout Drupal, we use a namespace common in PHP development; what it allows us to do is tell the framework where our class is located, and using autoloader, it will now look for our module and load the class we extend or implement.

In Drupal, we define the root as `\Drupal`; as you will notice, `\Drupal` is the root of the site, and after that it continues as the directory structure we have set out. However, you will notice that `src` is not shown in this; that's because the `src` directory contains the `global` namespace, the top level of all namespaces.

For our example, we will have a **Form** and a **Block**; these are both plugins in Drupal 8. Let's look at our namespace for Form.

`\Drupal\donate\Form`

As you can see, we have Drupal which is our root, donate which is our module name, and **Form**; instead of **Form**, we can have `Plugin\Block`, `Controller`, and `Services`.

Now that we understand how to structure our module, let's go ahead and create our **Form**.

What we need

For this bit of functionality, we will want to have a form that is inside a block. This is the basic functionality for this; upon submission, we want a donation to be created, which will then attach to our donations reference field that we created in our **fundraising** content type.

How we do it

First, we want to create our form; to do this, we need to create a `Form` directory inside our `src` directory. Once we have done this, we need to create a new **PHP Class**.

In PHPStorm, this can be done by right-clicking in the `Form` directory and selecting **New | PHP Class**.

We will then see a popup that has several fields to fill out:

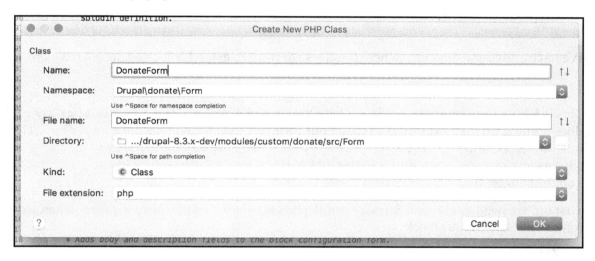

Fig 1.6: Create a Form class

What we have is the following:

- **Name**: This is the name of our **PHP Class**; it is also the name of our file without `.php`, as this is added automatically
- **Namespace**: This is how we know how to access the class from elsewhere in our site
- **File name**: This is the name of our **PHP Class**; it is also the name of our file without `.php`, as this is added automatically

If you are not using PHPStorm, you still need to follow the same principles in creating a new PHP file and naming it as `DonateForm.php`.

Now that we have our new class file created, we can see that it's a bit empty. First off, as we are creating a form, we need to extend our `FormBase` class; so to do this, we put the following:

```php
<?php

namespace Drupal\donate\Form;

use Drupal\Core\Form\FormBase;

class DonateForm extends FormBase {
}
```

We have added the directory where the class we want to extend is located, as we have our

`use Drupal\Core\Form\FormBase;`.

This is telling our `DonateForm` class where the class of `FormBase` is. Currently, our class does nothing, so the next step is to create our form; for this, we will need the `getFormId()`, `buildForm()`, and `submitForm()` methods. Also, there are other methods we can use, such as `validateForm()`, and the structure of this class can be found inside `/core/lib/Drupal/Core/Form/FormBase.php`.

First off, we need to give our form a form ID; this is how we can identify the form when we reference it later in our block:

```php
/**
 * {@inheritdoc}
 */
 public function getFormId()
{
      return 'user_donate_form';
 }
```

Now, create a new method called `buildForm()`; inside this, we will start building our form using the Drupal Form API.

This uses the `Drupal\Core\Form\FormStateInterface`, which is what we require for creating our form.

When we want to create or alter a form, we need to use the Form API to do so; this means we need to use an array. So, create a `buildForm()` method that will extend from the `Drupal\Core\Form\FormBase` class; we can extend or implement it due to the class being an `abstract` class:

```
/**
 * {@inheritdoc}
 */
public function buildForm(array $form, FormStateInterface $form_state) {
    $form['name'] = [
    '#type' => 'textfield',
    '#title' => $this->t('Your name'),
    '#required' => TRUE,
    '#description' => t('By default your username will show, you can
    however amend this.'),
    ];
    $form['mail'] = [
    '#type' => 'email',
    '#title' => $this->t('Your email'),
    '#disabled' => TRUE,
    ];
    $form['amount'] = [
    '#type' => 'textfield',
    '#title' => $this->t('Amount to pledge'),
    '#length' => 5,
    '#prefix' => '£',
    '#required' => TRUE,
    ];
    $form['submit'] = [
    '#type' => 'submit',
    '#value' => $this->t('Donate'),
    ];
    return $form;
}
```

What this will do is generate the form using our `FormBase` class, which we are extending.

If you want to learn more about the Form API, visit `https://api.drupal.org/api/drupal/elements/8.2.x`.

Now that we have done this, we have our form created and can access it anywhere in Drupal.

The next part of a form is the submit handler; we do this by adding a `submitForm()` method.

This takes arguments that we can use inside this method. If we want to display a value from the submitted form, then we will use $form_state.

What we will do now is just display a message saying **Donation added**; we will change this later when we make the form more complicated.

Creating a block

In Drupal 7, we will use hooks to create our blocks; as we have moved towards the OOP approach, this has thankfully been replaced. So, what we will do is create a block; in Drupal 8, these are known as plugins, as we can reuse them throughout Drupal.

Let's get our block built; all we want to do is allow our DonateForm to appear inside a block.

Create a new directory inside src called Plugin; this is where we can keep all our plugins for this module. We can further define it by making another directory inside Plugin called Block.

Inside this, we want to create our block class for our donation form block.

We will call our new class DonateBlock. Now that we have our new class, let's extend our BlockBase class:

```php
<?php

namespace Drupal\donate\Plugin\Block;

use Drupal\Core\Block\BlockBase;

class DonateBlock extends BlockBase {

}
```

Again, what we have done here is we extended our core class for the block plugin, and we are telling Drupal where our class for this is located.

Annotations

In Drupal 8 and Symfony, we use annotations as metadata; these appear to look as though they are comments, but we have some keywords that allow us to tell Drupal what the plugin is and what it does:

```
/**
 * Class DonateForm
 * @package Drupal\donate\Form
 *
 * @Block(
 *   id = "donate_block",
 *   admin_label = @Translation("Donation block"),
 *   category = @Translation("Custom")
 * )
 */
```

- `id`: This is our plugins, unique identifier.
- `admin_label`: This shows the title of the plugin.
- `category`: This shows which category our plugin is in.

The annotations are straightforward, but they are required for Drupal to know about the plugin.

We now need a method of `build()` that will then make our block. Inside this method, we want to locate the `form_id` and render it inside our block:

```
/**
 * {@inheritdoc}
 */
public function build() {
  $form = \Drupal::formBuilder()->getForm('\Drupal\donate\Form');

  return $form;
}
```

What we are doing here is creating a new instance of `formBuilder()` to get our method and pass the argument of where our `DonateForm` class is located. This will subsequently display our block. It's now time to see this in practice; remember that we just created a form inside a block, so after a quick cache rebuild, go to **Structure** | **Block layout.** We want our **Donate** block to appear under our Main page content.

We will only want this block to show on our **fundraising** page content type. Once all this has been done, click on **Save block**. Now, it's time to view our block with our donation form on our first **fundraising** page:

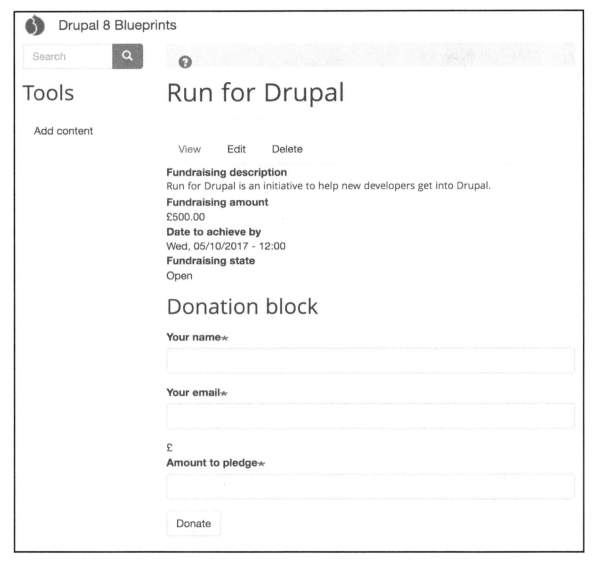

Fig 1.7: Donation form inside our block

Great stuff! You've just written your first custom module using a custom form inside its very own block.

Here's the full code we have just written:

```php
<?php
namespace Drupal\donate\Plugin\Block;
use Drupal\Core\Block\BlockBase;
/**
 * Class DonateForm
 * @package Drupal\donate\Form
 *
 * @Block(
 *    id = "donate_block",
 *    admin_label = @Translation("Donation block"),
 *    category = @Translation("Custom")
 * )
 */
class DonateBlock extends BlockBase {
/**
 * {@inheritdoc}
 */
 public function build()
 {
        $form = \Drupal::formBuilder()-
        >getForm('\Drupal\donate\Form\DonateForm');
        return $form;
    }
}
```

Now, we will add some extra complexity to this. If you are not logged in, we want a message to show instead of the form.

To do this, we will want to identify whether our current user is logged in and therefore an authenticated user.

To do this, we need to access our core Drupal class; if you want to take a look, head over to /core/lib/Drupal.php.

Inside this class, we have a method called currentUser(); this in turn uses Symfony's ContainerInterface.

Great! Now that we have a basic understanding of where this magic happens, we will now check whether the user is an authenticated user.

To do this, we use the following:

```
\Drupal::currentUser()->isAuthenticated()
```

This simply returns a TRUE or FALSE statement. We can access the currentUser() object at any time just using \Drupal::currentUser().

By default, we want to show the logged in user details; to do this, we use #default_value in the Form API:

```
/**
 * {@inheritdoc}
 */
public function buildForm(array $form, FormStateInterface $form_state)
{
        $user = \Drupal::currentUser();
        if ($user->isAuthenticated())
        {
                $form['name'] = [
                '#type' => 'textfield',
                '#title' => $this->t('Your name'),
                '#required' => TRUE,
                '#description' => t('By default your username will show,
                you can however amend this.'),
                '#default_value' => $user->getDisplayName(),
                ];
                $form['mail'] = [
                '#type' => 'email',
                '#title' => $this->t('Your email'),
                '#default_value' => $user->getEmail(),
                '#disabled' => TRUE,
                ];
                $form['amount'] = [
                '#type' => 'textfield',
                '#title' => $this->t('Amount to pledge'),
                '#length' => 5,
                '#prefix' => '£',
                '#required' => TRUE,
                ];
                $form['submit'] = [
                '#type' => 'submit',
                '#value' => $this->t('Donate'),
                ];
        }
        else
```

```
    {
            drupal_set_message(t('You must be logged in to donate.'),
            'error');
    }
return $form;
}
```

As can be seen here, we have added some default values, which just means that a value is shown in the field by default.

We have also made it easier to access the user object by setting it as a variable of $user.

When we set up our donation content type, we only used one new field, which was the donation amount. We have a user ID field that is default to content types; this way, we can tell what the user's email and name is.

Creating a node programmatically

Inside our submitForm() method we want to take the values from $form_state, this tracks the current state of the form, where its build, processed, validated and submitted.

$form state object

As $form_state is now an object; we no longer need to use arrays to get the values we need.

To get an individual value from the form we will use $form_state->getValue('field_name'); this looks a lot nicer than what we previously had to do in Drupal 7.

So, let's create our submitForm() method and take the values we need from our form submission.

```
/**
 * {@inheritdoc}
 */
public function submitForm(array &$form, FormStateInterface
$form_state)
{
    // Get submitted form values.
    $name = $form_state->getValue('name');
    $amount = $form_state->getValue('amount');
```

```
        // Display a thank you message.
        drupal_set_message(t('Thank you for the donation of %amount. ',
        array('%amount' => $amount)));
}
```

In the preceding code, we are simply going to start off by showing a thank you message with the amount value from the form submission. Using the `getValue()` to take our individual field value, we then make it into a variable. We then pass the value into our `drupal_set_message()` inside `t()`, which we use to allow text to be translated if we want to. Note, however, that we don't actually put a variable inside the `t()`, instead we use a placeholder which is either a `%`, `!` or `@`.

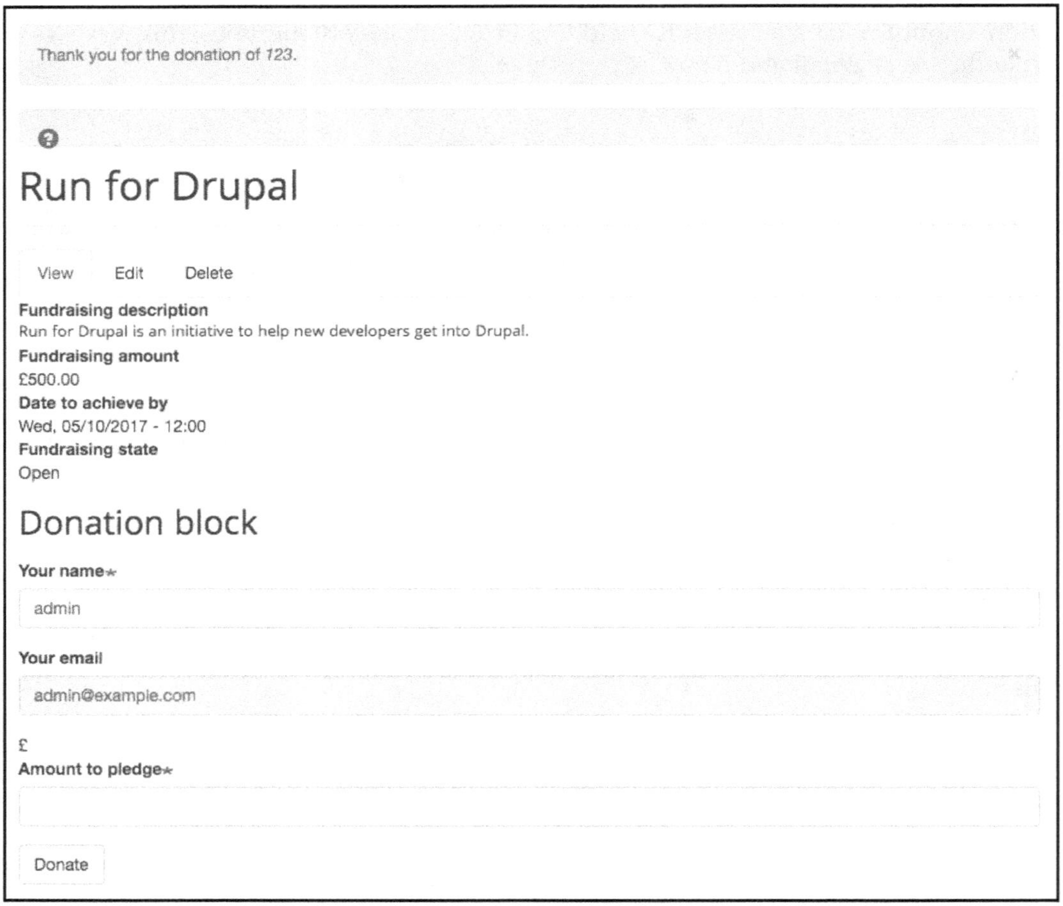

Thank you for the donation of *123*.

❷

Run for Drupal

View   Edit   Delete

Fundraising description
Run for Drupal is an initiative to help new developers get into Drupal.
Fundraising amount
£500.00
Date to achieve by
Wed, 05/10/2017 - 12:00
Fundraising state
Open

Donation block

Your name★

admin

Your email

admin@example.com

£
Amount to pledge★

Donate

Fig 1.8: Donation success message

As we can see in *Fig 1.8*, our form has been submitted, and it is now showing that we have donated 123. However, this hasn't actually really done anything, and when we reload the page, nothing will have been saved.

Now we want to create our donation content; to do this, we need to use Node::create():

```
// Create a donation node.
$donation = Node::create(['type' => 'donation']);
$donation->set('title', 'Donation' . time());
$donation->set('field_donation_amount', $amount);
$donation->set('field_name', $name);
$donation->set('uid', \Drupal::currentUser()->id());
$donation->enforceIsNew();
$donation->save();
```

So, to make our life easier, we will name this $donation.

Here's what is happening here:

1. Tell Drupal the content type we want to create.
2. Set the title of our new node.
3. Set which fields we want to add values to.
4. Use our currentUser() object and get the current logged in user's user ID, so they are the author of our node.
5. Ensure that the node is new before saving.
6. Save our node.

This is a nice, straightforward and clean looking approach to creating a new node programmatically.

As we have now created our first donation, we now want to assign it to our fundraising page. To do this, we need to use Drupal's routing system \Drupal::routeMatch()->getParameter('node');.

This converts the parameter of the node and gets the node ID for our fundraising page. Now that we have our node ID, we will load our node object and update the donation nid into our donations field:

```
// Attach donation to fundraising node.
$fundraising_page = \Drupal::routeMatch()->getParameter('node');
$fundraising_nid = $fundraising_page->id();
$fundraising_node = Node::load($fundraising_nid);
$fundraising_node->field_donations[] = ['target_id' => $donation_nid];
$fundraising_node->save();
```

Here's what is happening:

1. Get the current node ID based on the path.
2. Load our node object from our node ID.
3. Update our donation into our entity reference field.
4. Save our donation to our fundraising page.

As our field is a multivalue, we need to `add []` after our field name, as its acting as an array, and we then set the value of the `target_id`:

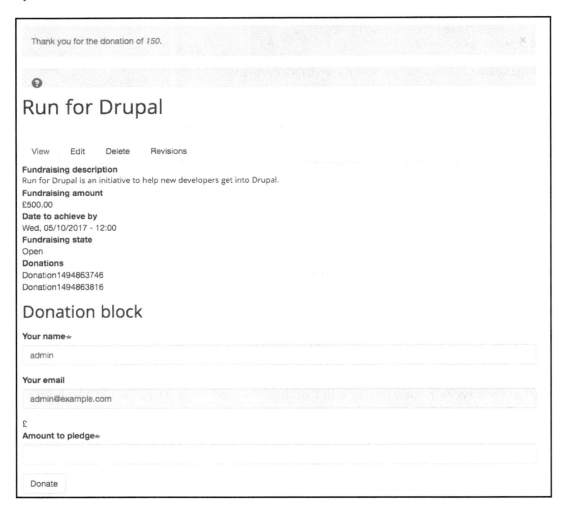

Fig 1.9: Donations attached to our fundraising page

Now, if we go back and submit the form again, we will see that our donation is added.

So, once the donation is submitted, we want to send a thank you message to our donator; to do this, we will send an email.

Sending emails

To send an email, we need to access the `MailManager`, which is a plugin in Drupal.

In order to do this, we need to go back to our `DonateForm` and access our service; in this case, we want to access our mail service:

```
$mail_manager = \Drupal::service('plugin.manager.mail');
```

What this does is that it allows us to load Drupal's `MailManager` service, that will allow us to send our email to our donator.

After we've called the service, we need to pass some values into the service:

```
$to = \Drupal::currentUser()->getEmail();
 $params['message'] = t('Thanks @name for donating towards our
%fundraising_title.',
   array('@name' => $name, '%fundraising_title' =>
$fundraising_node->getTitle()));

 $mail_manager->mail('donate', 'donation_submitted', $to, $langcode,
$params,  NULL, TRUE);
```

What we are doing here is getting our user's email address, defining a message with two values, and then submitting the email; however, this won't send anything as we are missing `hook_mail()`, which we need to pass all the values in order for it to send.

In order to send an email, we need to create a new module file; so, in the `root` of this module, create `donate.module`.

donate.module

```
<?php
/**
 * @file
 * Donate module.
 */

/**
```

```
 * Implements hook_mail().
 */
function donate_mail($key, &$message, $params) {
  $message['from'] = Drupal::config('system.site')->get('mail');
  $message['subject'] = t('Thanks for donating!');
  $message['body'][] = $params['message'];
}
```

Simply, we are invoking this hook to pass our parameters from our
`MailManagerInterface()`, which is from our `MailManager` service. Now that we have
done this, we will get an email and a thank you message when we submit our form.

Congratulations, you have just created a node, and attached the newly created node to an
existing node.

So, we have just allowed donations to be submitted and assigned to our fundraising page;
let's just hide the donations from this page.

Next, we will write some more code in a module that will show our current amount
donated compared to our amount required.

Donation progress bar

For the next part, we will create a progress bar using the HTML5 `<progress>` attribute. To
do this, we need to create a module that will calculate all the amounts we have and show it
inside a `twig` template inside a block.

Start off by creating a new module called `donation_progress`.

donation_progressinfo.yml

```
name: Donation progress
description: Displays a progress bar of current donations
core: 8.x
type: module
package: Donate
```

Then, create a `Block` plugin again, so `src/Plugin/Block`; we will create a new class for
our block called `DonateRangeBlock`.

DonateRangeBlock.php

As we did previously, we will extend our BlockBase class, add our annotations, and add our build() method:

```php
<?php

namespace Drupal\donate_range\Plugin\Block;

use Drupal\Core\Block\BlockBase;

/**
 * Class DonateRangeBlock
 * @package Drupal\donate_range\Form
 *
 * @Block(
 *   id = "donate_range_block",
 *   admin_label = @Translation("Donation range block"),
 *   category = @Translation("Custom")
 * )
 */
class DonateRangeBlock extends BlockBase {

  /**
   * {@inheritdoc}
   */
  public function build() {

  }

}
```

So now, we're at a starting place to add our functionality into this block.

First, we want to get the current node ID. So, inside our build() method, we need to add the following:

```php
$nid = \Drupal::routeMatch()->getParameter('node')->id();
$node = Node::load($nid);
```

Now that we have our node object, we want to get two fields of data. First off, we want to get the amount the fundraiser wants to reach, and then we want to get all the donation amounts.

To get the value of a field, we use `get('field_name')->value;`:

```
$target_amount = $node->get('field_fundraising_amount')->value;
```

This will simply return our rendered value.

As we now want all the donation amounts, we must remember that this uses entity reference, so the only value available to us is the donation node ID, which we can use to get the field value for that node.

So, to do this, we use the following:

```
$nids = $node->field_donations->getValue();
```

This returns our donations node IDs into an array, and as we want to add up each donation, we need to create a loop:

```
$donations = array();
 // Take all our referenced nids.
 foreach ($nids as $donation) {
   $donation_id = Node::load($donation['target_id']);
   $donations[] = $donation_id->get('field_donation_amount')->value;
 }
```

What we are doing here is starting an empty array of `$donations` and then looping each within the array of `nids` from our donations.

From inside the loop, again we want to load our node based on the `nid` and then get our specific donation amount. As we are putting this all into an array, we can add the values up very easily.

We will return a simple result with some text and render this onto the page:

```
return [
   '#markup' => $this->t('We have received £%donations of £%target',
     array(
       '%donations' => $donations_received,
       '%target' => $target_amount,
     )
   ),
 ];
```

What we are doing here is taking our values and outputting them into our block. If we cache rebuild, then we will see the block displaying our new content:

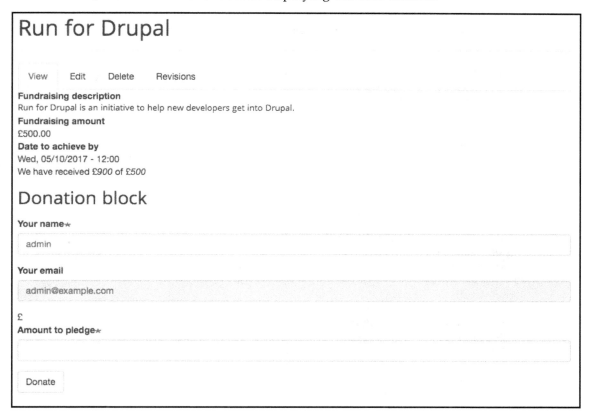

Fig 1.10 : Our donation block showing what's been raised

In *Fig 1.10*, the fundraising content type has been tidied up a bit, and our Donation range amount is now showing.

However, it doesn't look that attractive, so what we will do next is make this editable for our themer.

DonateRangeBlock.php

```php
<?php

namespace Drupal\donate_range\Plugin\Block;
use Drupal\node\Entity\Node;
```

```
use Drupal\Core\Block\BlockBase;

/**
 * Class DonateRangeBlock
 * @package Drupal\donate_range\Form
 *
 * @Block(
 *   id = "donate_range_block",
 *   admin_label = @Translation("Donation range block"),
 *   category = @Translation("Custom")
 * )
 */
class DonateRangeBlock extends BlockBase {

  /**
   * {@inheritdoc}
   */
  public function build() {

    $nid = \Drupal::routeMatch()->getParameter('node')->id();
    $node = Node::load($nid);
    $target_amount = $node->get('field_fundraising_amount')->value;
    $nids = $node->field_donations->getValue();
    $donations = array();
    // Take all our referenced nids.
    foreach ($nids as $donation) {
      $donation_id = Node::load($donation['target_id']);
      $donations[] = $donation_id->get('field_donation_amount')->value;
    }
    // Add up all donations.
    $donations_received = array_sum($donations);

    return [
      '#markup' => $this->t('We have received £%donations of £%target',
        array(
          '%donations' => $donations_received,
          '%target' => $target_amount,
        )
      ),
    ];
  }

}
```

Theming our plugin

Our next step is to make our block content themable. To do this, we need to create a hook, which you may recognize from Drupal 7. So, let's create a `donate_range.module` file in the root of our module.

Next, we will use `hook_theme()` to declare our theme for our `twig` template:

```php
<?php
/**
 * @file
 * Donation progress.
 */

/**
 * Implements hook_theme().
 */
function donate_range_theme($existing, $type, $theme, $path) {
  return [
    'donate_range' => [
      'variables' => [
        'amount' => NULL,
        'donations' => NULL
      ],
    ],
  ];
}
```

Now that this has been done, we can go back to our `DonateRangeBlock.php` file and apply this.

DonateRangeBlock.php

We returned our markup with our message earlier, but we will now replace this with our template name and its variables that we declared in our module file:

```php
return [
    '#theme' => 'donate_range',
    '#amount'=> $target_amount,
    '#donations' => $donations_received,
];
```

So, what this does is that it tells Drupal that we want to use our `donate_range` template, and we want to declare the values of the variables we created in our module.

Now, if you cache rebuild, you won't see anything where the donation amount text was displayed; this is because there is no template for Drupal to use.

What we will now do is create a themeable template and use the values we are returning inside of it.

Our Twig variables are exactly as they are declared in the preceding return, apart from the #.

donate-range.html.twig

You may have noticed that we don't use an underscore in our Twig templates, so the underscore in `donate_range` will change to `donate-progress`, and we will add `.html.twig` to the end of it.

Add our original message, but let's wrap it inside a paragraph tag, `<p>`:

```
{#
/**
 * @file
 * Donation range widget template.
 */
#}

<p>We have received &pound;{{ donations }} of &pound;{{ amount }}</p>
```

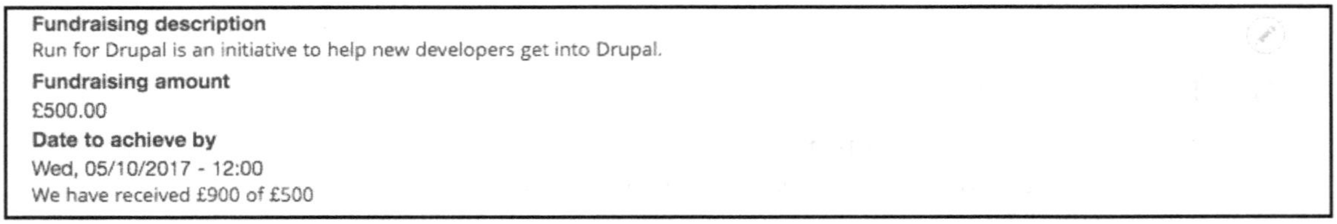

Fundraising description
Run for Drupal is an initiative to help new developers get into Drupal.
Fundraising amount
£500.00
Date to achieve by
Wed, 05/10/2017 - 12:00
We have received £900 of £500

Fig 1.11

As can be seen in *Fig 1.11*, we can now see our template output on our **fundraising** page.

Now, we will use the HTML5 `<progress>` attribute to show a simple progress bar. We will also use `{% trans %}` in `twig` to allow our paragraph to be translatable through Drupal:

```
{#
/**
```

```
 * @file
 * Donation range widget template.
 */
#}

<p>
{% trans %}
    We have received &pound;{{ donations }} of &pound;{{ amount }}
{% endtrans %}
</p>

<progress max="{{ amount }}" value="{{ donations }}"></progress>
```

The preceding code allows us to use a paragraph of text and our `twig` variables inside it; it's also allowing us to make the entire paragraph translatable, which we will cover later.

If we save this, cache rebuild, and reload this page, we will see the progress bar we have just created:

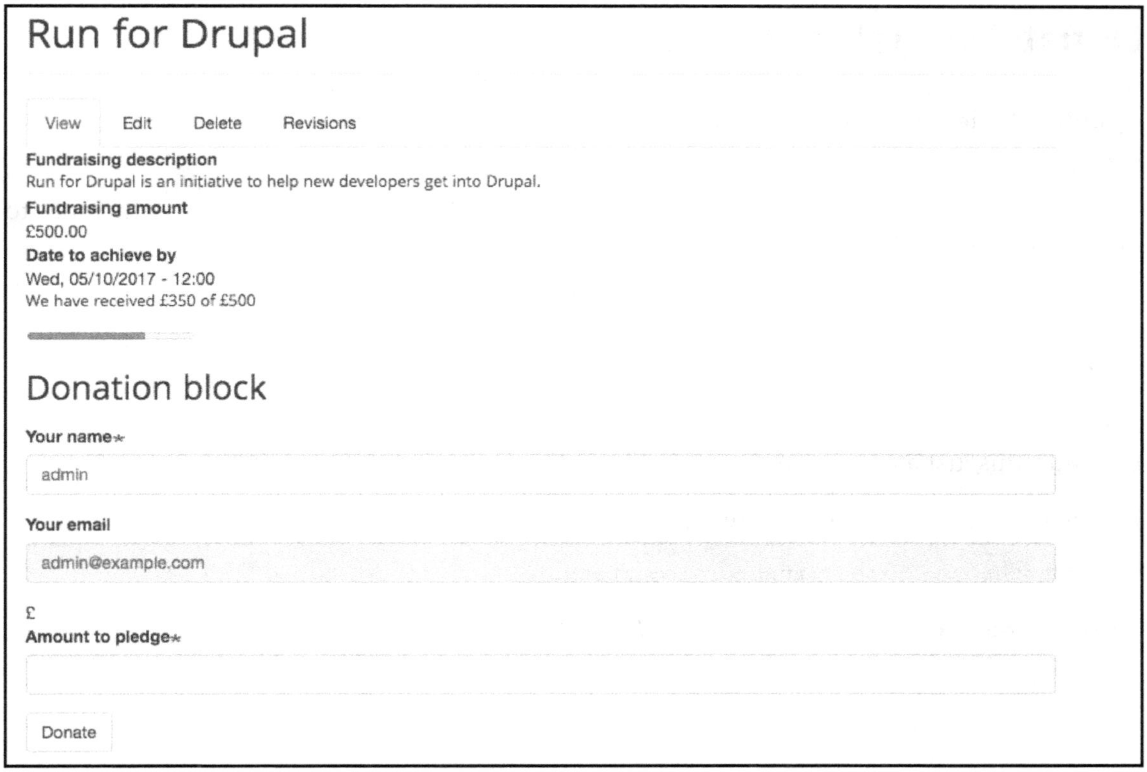

Run for Drupal

View   Edit   Delete   Revisions

Fundraising description
Run for Drupal is an initiative to help new developers get into Drupal.
Fundraising amount
£500.00
Date to achieve by
Wed, 05/10/2017 - 12:00
We have received £350 of £500

Donation block

Your name✶

admin

Your email

admin@example.com

£
Amount to pledge✶

Donate

Fig 1.12: Progress bar showing amounts

We now have a basic fundraising page that shows how much has been donated and what the target is; this is being displayed as a progress bar.

To finish this chapter off, we will amend some of the code we have just written; we have covered it all before in this chapter, so it shouldn't be too difficult to do.

Finishing off

So, we have our donation and fundraising content type, fundraiser dashboard, custom form to submit a donation, send email after donation has been submitted, and our donation range block.

However, what happens if the fundraising goal has been reached now? We can decide to keep the ability to submit a donation there, or for this example, we will hide the form and show a message saying that the donation has been reached.

DonateRangeBlock.php

If the value has been reached, we want to add a variable to our theme that we can use as a condition to determine whether we show the progress of the fundraising or if we just show a message.

We will then update the status of the **fundraising** page to **Closed**, which we will then use to determine whether the donation form is to be shown:

```
if ($donations_received >= $target_amount) {
  $node->field_fundraising_state = 1;
  $node->save();
  $fundraising_status = TRUE;
}
```

Let's add this just after `$donations_received = array_sum($donations);`.

Inside our return statement, we want to add another variable:

```
'#status' => isset($fundraising_status) ? 1 : '',
```

So, our `DonateRangeBlock` class should now look like this:

```
<?php

namespace Drupal\donate_range\Plugin\Block;
use Drupal\node\Entity\Node;
```

```php
use Drupal\Core\Block\BlockBase;

/**
 * Class DonateRangeBlock
 * @package Drupal\donate_range\Form
 *
 * @Block(
 *   id = "donate_range_block",
 *   admin_label = @Translation("Donation range block"),
 *   category = @Translation("Custom")
 * )
 */
class DonateRangeBlock extends BlockBase {

  /**
   * {@inheritdoc}
   */
  public function build() {

    $nid = \Drupal::routeMatch()->getParameter('node')->id();
    $node = Node::load($nid);
    $target_amount = $node->get('field_fundraising_amount')->value;
    $nids = $node->field_donations->getValue();
    $donations = array();
    // Take all our referenced nids.
    foreach ($nids as $donation) {
      $donation_id = Node::load($donation['target_id']);
      $donations[] = $donation_id->get('field_donation_amount')->value;
    }
    // Add up all donations.
    $donations_received = array_sum($donations);

    // Check if target has been reached.
    if ($donations_received >= $target_amount) {
      $node->field_fundraising_state = 1;
      $node->save();
      $fundraising_status = TRUE;
    }

    return [
      '#theme' => 'donate_range',
      '#amount'=> $target_amount,
      '#donations' => $donations_received,
      '#status' => isset($fundraising_status) ? 1 : '',
    ];
  }

}
```

What you may also have noticed is that the donations don't update until we do a cache rebuild; this is because our block is currently cached. So, in order to stop it from caching, we will add another method--`getCacheMaxAge()`--and we will set it to 0:

```
/**
 * {@inheritdoc}
 */
public function getCacheMaxAge() {
  return 0;
}
```

Now, we need to go back to `donate_range.module` and update our `hook_theme()`. We need to add `'status' => NULL`:

```php
<?php
/**
 * @file
 * Donation progress.
 */

/**
 * Implements hook_theme().
 */
function donate_range_theme($existing, $type, $theme, $path) {
  return [
    'donate_range' => [
      'variables' => [
        'amount' => NULL,
        'donations' => NULL,
        'status' => NULL
      ],
    ],
  ];
}
```

Right, so we have our additional variable added to our `hook_theme()` and our block. Let's go and add this, with some conditions, into our template.

donate-range.html.twig

We will now look at using conditional statements in Twig.

Conditions are done using this:

```
{% if variable condition %}
  Show something
{% else %}
  Show something else
{% endif %}
```

So, to put this into practice, we will check whether the status variable is empty, which means the **fundraising** page is still open, and the fundraising target hasn't been reached.

However, if it has been reached, we will show a message saying that it's been reached:

```
{#
/**
 * @file
 * Donation range widget template.
 */
#}

{% if status is empty %}
    <p>
        {% trans %}
        We have received &pound;{{ donations }} of &pound;{{ amount }}
        {% endtrans %}
    </p>

    <progress max="{{ amount }}" value="{{ donations }}"></progress>
{% else %}
    <p>
        {% trans %}
            Thanks our donation target has been reached.
        {% endtrans %}
    </p>
{% endif %}
```

Finally, we will go into our donation form and add an amend to not show the form if the target donation is met.

DonateForm.php

We will simply get our node ID, and then the status of the **fundraising** page, and we will
show the form depending on that.

Add this just beneath our `$user` variable inside `buildForm()`:

```
$nid = \Drupal::routeMatch()->getParameter('node')->id();
$node = Node::load($nid);
$status = $node->field_fundraising_state->value;
```

Then, add a condition around the entire `$form` array that will only show if the status `!= 1`,
which is our Boolean for our closed **fundraising** page:

```
/**
 * {@inheritdoc}
 */
public function buildForm(array $form, FormStateInterface $form_state) {
    $user = \Drupal::currentUser();
    $nid = \Drupal::routeMatch()->getParameter('node')->id();
    $node = Node::load($nid);
    $status = $node->field_fundraising_state->value;
    if ($user->isAuthenticated())
    {
        if ($status != 1)
        {
            $form['name'] = [
            '#type' => 'textfield',
            '#title' => $this->t('Your name'),
            '#required' => TRUE,
            '#description' => t('By default your username will show,
            you can however amend this.'),
            '#default_value' => $user->getAccountName(),
            ];
            $form['mail'] = [
            '#type' => 'email',
            '#title' => $this->t('Your email'),
            '#default_value' => $user->getEmail(),
            '#disabled' => TRUE,
            ];
            $form['amount'] = [
            '#type' => 'textfield',
            '#title' => $this->t('Amount to pledge'),
            '#length' => 5,
            '#prefix' => '£',
            '#required' => TRUE,
            ];
            $form['submit'] = [
```

```
              '#type' => 'submit',
              '#value' => $this->t('Donate'),
            ];
        }
        else
        {
            drupal_set_message(t('Thanks our donation target has
            been reached.'), 'status');
        }
    }
    else
    {
        drupal_set_message(t('You must be logged in to donate.'),
        'error');
    }

    return $form;
}
```

So now we have added this extra functionality to our **fundraising** page, you have now learned:

- Creating a simple user dashboard with views
- Understanding how user permissions work
- Account management
- Basics of creating a module
- Creating and updating a node
- Creating block plugins
- Creating and submitting forms
- Sending emails
- Using field values to do some math
- Making templates for our module to be used in the frontend

We will use similar aspects of this throughout the rest of the book, but we have really gone into the deep end and got stuck into some Drupal 8 coding, and its doing quite a bit just by using Drupal API and the Symfony framework.

In the next chapter we will look at how to make a job recruitment website; in this chapter we will start to look at a new way to manage your Drupal website using Composer, and creating multiple user roles with different fields to register and assign them to users.

4

Recruit Using Drupal

With any business, recruitment is very important. There are many well-known recruitment platforms out there that allow you to just upload your CV, create a profile, and wait to be contacted. However, from a recruiter's perspective, there is the ability to also create your company profile and create jobs.

In this chapter, we will look at creating a recruitment website that allows a candidate to create a profile and apply for jobs by searching for jobs and getting search results.

We will also look at making the recruiter part where they can post jobs and get a log of when a candidate has applied for a job.

We will cover the following throughout this chapter:

- Look at a new technique to install Drupal and add additional functionality
- Create multiple user roles
- Look at how to add fields to the registration form
- Create a user role that is autoassigned to our newly registered user
- Look at a Webform module and how we can use it

Getting started

As we are building a new website, we need to reinstall Drupal; ensure that you save your database from the last chapter.

Before we do that, we will introduce a new technique for this. In Drupal 8, Composer was introduced instead of what we previously had, which was `.make` files.

What is Composer?

First off, Composer is awesome! Composer allows us to manage dependencies required for an application; these dependencies are stored on packagist (`https://packagist.org`).

However, you can also define your own private repository for your custom dependencies.

When we use Composer, we can easily update our dependencies to the latest version; this keeps all our packages inside a `vendor` directory.

To install Composer, visit: `https://getcomposer.org/doc/00-intro.md`.

To start off Composer, the command will be `composer [command]`.

When we use Composer, we will have a `composer.json` file, which is simply an empty JSON file. Then, we use a command called `require`. What this command does is to add a line that tells Composer *Hey I want this package, can you get me it* into our `composer.json` file.

Once we require a package, we can update it using `composer update`. This checks the repository for the latest release of that package.

Drupal has its own Composer repository, and this is great as it makes managing a Drupal site even easier. We then have more control over what contrib we want to use, and this also means that it's less likely to be modified. This is because we have a field called `composer.lock` that keeps all the information on which packages and versions are being used, which in turn will mean there will be no discrepancies when working on a project.

Using Composer with Drupal

To get started with using Composer with Drupal, create a new directory and then head over to that directory within the command line.

The command used to create a new Drupal project using `composer` is as follows:

```
composer create-project drupal-composer/drupal-project:8.x-dev some-dir --
stability dev --no-interaction
```

What this does is create a new directory and set up our Drupal site structure. We will now execute the preceding command, and then Composer will run tasks to get all the packages needed. This is illustrated here:

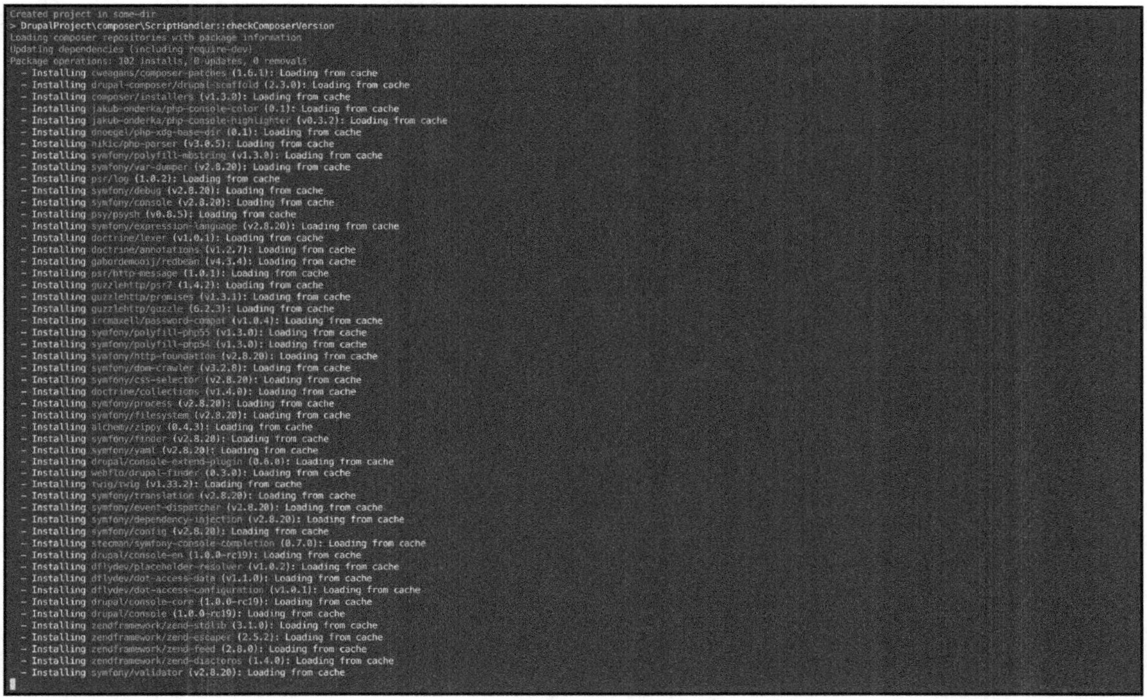

Fig 1.0: Composer downloading dependencies for Drupal

In the preceding screenshot, we can see Composer getting all the dependencies we will need for Drupal:

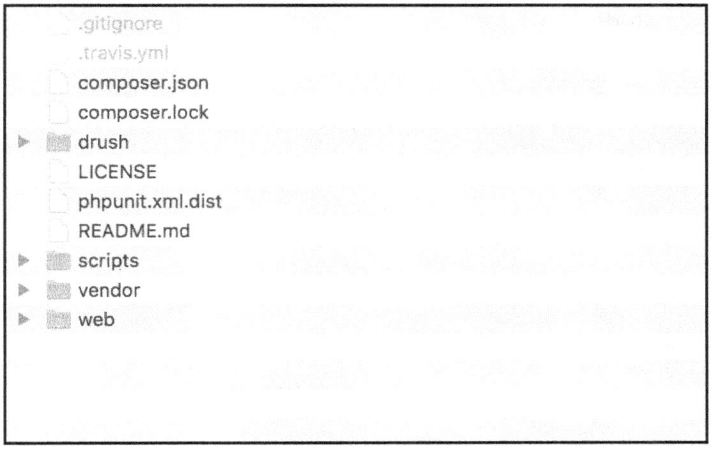

Fig 1.1: Directory structure after Composer is executed

As we can see in the preceding screenshot, Composer has run and executed the script, and our application structure is all there. We can see that there is a composer.json file, which has been generated from our composer create-project command. A part of the composer.json file is shown in the following screenshot:

```
{
    "name": "drupal-composer/drupal-project",
    "description": "Project template for Drupal 8 projects with composer",
    "type": "project",
    "license": "GPL-2.0+",
    "authors": [
        {
            "name": "",
            "role": ""
        }
    ],
    "repositories": [
        {
            "type": "composer",
            "url": "https://packages.drupal.org/8"
        }
    ],
    "require": {
        "composer/installers": "^1.2",
        "cweagans/composer-patches": "^1.6",
        "drupal-composer/drupal-scaffold": "^2.2",
        "drupal/console": "~1.0",
        "drupal/core": "~8.0",
        "drush/drush": "~8.0",
        "webflo/drupal-finder": "^0.3.0",
        "webmozart/path-util": "^2.3"
    },
    "require-dev": {
        "behat/mink": "~1.7",
        "behat/mink-goutte-driver": "~1.2",
        "jcalderonzumba/gastonjs": "~1.0.2",
        "jcalderonzumba/mink-phantomjs-driver": "~0.3.1",
        "mikey179/vfsstream": "~1.2",
        "phpunit/phpunit": ">=4.8.28 <5",
        "symfony/css-selector": "~2.8"
    },
    "conflict": {
        "drupal/drupal": "*"
    },
    "minimum-stability": "dev",
    "prefer-stable": true,
    "config": {
      "sort-packages": true
    },
    "autoload": {
        "classmap": [
            "scripts/composer/ScriptHandler.php"
        ]
    },
    "scripts": {
        "drupal-scaffold": "DrupalComposer\\DrupalScaffold\\Plugin::scaffold",
        "pre-install-cmd": [
            "DrupalProject\\composer\\ScriptHandler::checkComposerVersion"
        ],
        "pre-update-cmd": [
            "DrupalProject\\composer\\ScriptHandler::checkComposerVersion"
```

Fig 1.3: Part of the composer.json file

This is the structure of our `composer.json` file, and as can be seen, it's in a JSON structure. So now, we have our Drupal site built using Composer, which we can add to our development environment.

If we want to add a module to our Drupal site, instead of `drush` or `drupal console`, we can simply use `composer require drupal/devel`. What this does is that it makes `devel` a required module and will download it to our `contrib` directory inside our `/web` directory:

```
"extra": {
    "installer-paths": {
        "web/core": ["type:drupal-core"],
        "web/libraries/{$name}": ["type:drupal-library"],
        "web/modules/contrib/{$name}": ["type:drupal-module"],
        "web/profiles/contrib/{$name}": ["type:drupal-profile"],
        "web/themes/contrib/{$name}": ["type:drupal-theme"],
        "drush/contrib/{$name}": ["type:drupal-drush"]
    }
}
```

Fig 1.4: Directory structure for Drupal

The location of Drupal and our non-core plugins (modules, themes, profiles, and libraries) is set in the preceding screenshot. So, when we run an update for Composer or download any additional plugins, they will go in these directories.

So now that we understand Composer, we can move on to using Composer in the next chapter.

What we need

We will try and harness the power of Drupal core with minimal contrib modules and a small bit of custom code.

On this site, we will have two user roles: Recruiter and Candidate.

There will be a separate registration page for this, and we will be using the great Registration types (`https://drupal.org/project/registration_types`) module to achieve this. What this module allows us to do is to create individual registration pages for registering users and then autoassign a user role of our choice to that user. This is done by creating a view mode and then assigning it to our registration form; it also allows us to control which fields are shown to the user.

Now, download and install our `registration_types` module and enable it. Once this is done, we want to create two new roles:

- **Recruiter**
- **Candidate**

Go to **People** | **Roles** and click on **+ Add role**; previously, we used the default roles, but for this we want our user to be either a **Candidate** or **Recruiter**:

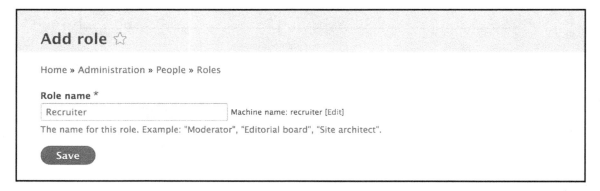

Fig 1.5: Add user role

In the preceding screenshot, we can see that our machine name is autogenerated like other parts in Drupal.

Once we click on **Save**, the user role is created and given a role ID, which is referenced throughout Drupal as a `rid`:

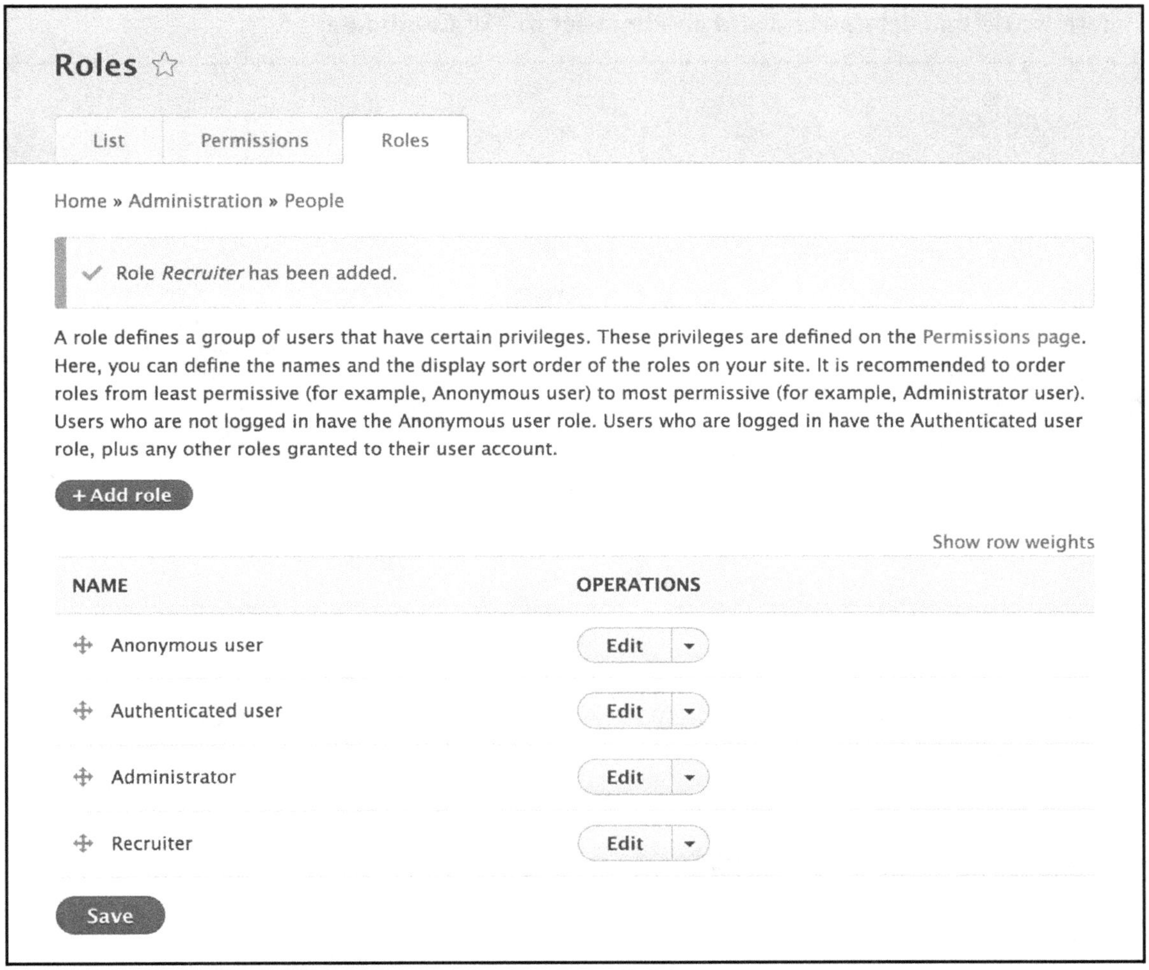

Roles ☆

List	Permissions	Roles

Home » Administration » People

> ✓ Role *Recruiter* has been added.

A role defines a group of users that have certain privileges. These privileges are defined on the Permissions page. Here, you can define the names and the display sort order of the roles on your site. It is recommended to order roles from least permissive (for example, Anonymous user) to most permissive (for example, Administrator user). Users who are not logged in have the Anonymous user role. Users who are logged in have the Authenticated user role, plus any other roles granted to their user account.

+ Add role

Show row weights

NAME	OPERATIONS
✛ Anonymous user	Edit ▾
✛ Authenticated user	Edit ▾
✛ Administrator	Edit ▾
✛ Recruiter	Edit ▾

Save

Fig 1.6: Use role order

Now that we have saved our new role, we can see it in our `draggable` table. The roles are ordered descending from the lowest level of access to the top. As **Recruiter** is appearing higher than **Administrator**, move **Recruiter** up one place so that **Administrator** is at the bottom. This will now show our **Permissions** page with our new user role.

Before we do that, let's go and add another user role of **Candidate**:

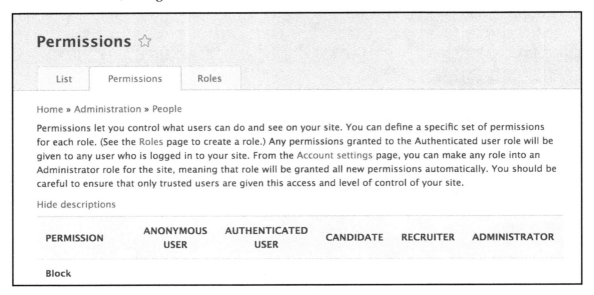

Fig 1.7: Permissions

As can be seen in the preceding screenshot, we can now see that our new two roles are displayed. This means that, through the permissions matrix, we can now assign our permissions for this user role.

Creating user registration pages

Now that we have got our new user roles added, we will use the `registration_types` contrib module.

We will create two view modes: one is for candidates and the other is for recruiters. To do this, we need to go to **Account settings**, which is inside **Configuration**.

Go to **Configuration | People**, and from here, you will see several tabs; we want to add fields for our registration form, so click on **Manage form display**. This page has the same layout as our content types; move down to **Custom display settings** and click on **Manage form modes**:

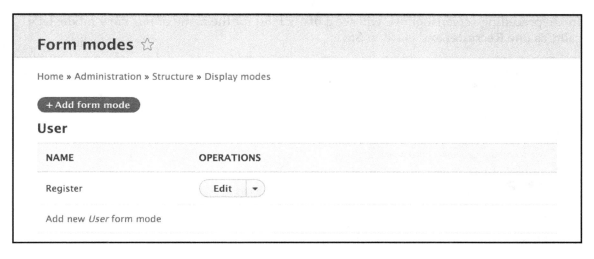

Fig 1.8: Manage form modes

Let's now create two view modes:

- **Candidate** registration
- **Recruiter** registration

In the preceding screenshot, we can see a view mode of **Register.** This is the default view mode set. We want to add two separate view modes and delete the **Register** one. Click on **Add new** *User* **form mode**:

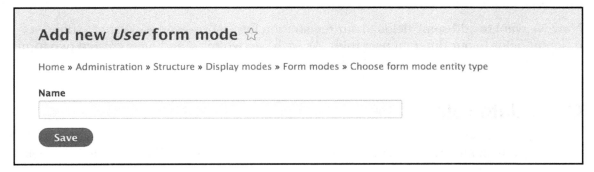

Fig 1.9: User form view mode

In the preceding screenshot, we will see a blank field for the name of our view mode; let's call this one **Recruiter** and click on **Save**:

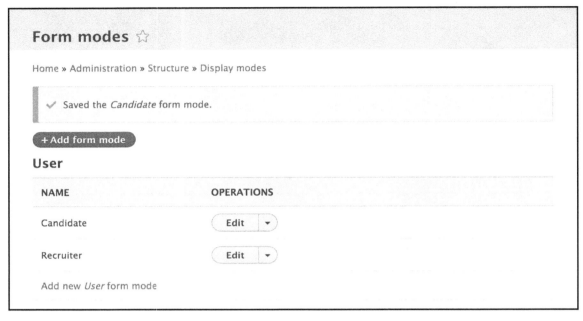

Fig 1.10: List of our form modes

Repeat this process for **Candidate**; once we have done this, our list should look like the preceding screenshot.

Now we want to add some fields to our registration forms; however, we want to show different fields to our different user roles. As we have two roles, and have created two form modes for our user roles, let's go ahead and add some fields.

Candidate role

The candidate is someone applying for a job. We need to have some fields that will set out what they are looking for so that the recruiter can see when the candidate applied for a job.

The fields we will create are as mentioned:

- **First name**: Textfield
- **Last name**: Textfield
- **Telephone no.**: Telephone (this module needs to be enabled)

- **Address**: Address (`https://drupal.org/project/address`)
- **Website**: Textfield
- **Contract type**: Taxonomy term reference
- **Job title**: Taxonomy term reference
- **Skills**: Taxonomy term reference
- **Desired Location**: Taxonomy term reference
- **Profile photo**: Image
- **CV**: File upload

These fields will be enough information required for a recruiter to see and also, for our candidate's profile to be viewable by the recruiters.

Firstly, let's download the address module (`https://drupal.org/project/address`). As we are using Composer, we need to add it as a dependency:

```
composer require drupal/address
```

Now that we have downloaded the address module, we need to enable it; what this does to create a new field type that we can use throughout the site,and which we will use on our profile.

So, we are all set to start setting up our candidate profile; let's go and create our **Type of contract** taxonomy. Refreshing our memory, let's go to **Admin** | **Structure** | **Taxonomy** and create a taxonomy vocabulary called **Type of contract**.

Repeat the creation of taxonomy vocabularies for the following:

- Job title
- Skills
- Preferred location

The reason we have created these three taxonomy vocabularies is so that we can use them for better categorization, and we can allow previously created terms to be reused by the users.

Now that we have done this, let's go back to **Account settings** and add our fields. We will be using the same fields for the different registrations and enabling our view modes. The enabling of view modes is shown in the next screenshot:

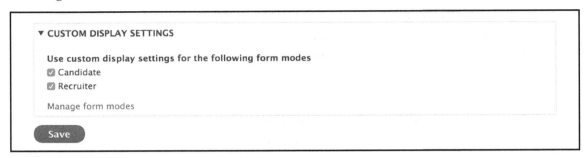

Fig 1.12: Enable view modes

In *Fig 1.12*, we can see our different display settings that are available to us to enable.

This is how we will determine what fields will show on the different registration forms. This then creates two tabs. We will now set out how our form is displayed for candidates. We will also use **field group** (https://drupal.org/project/field_group) to organize our fields on the form to make it readable.

Once this module is enabled, go back to **Account settings** and then to **Manage form display**. Once you are on this page, click on **Candidate** for our view mode; this will take us to our **Candidate** specific fields, and then click on **+ Add group**. We will now split this form into two groups.

Then, select **Fieldset** and give it a label of **Personal details**, and click on **Save and continue**. The field group settings are shown in the following screenshot:

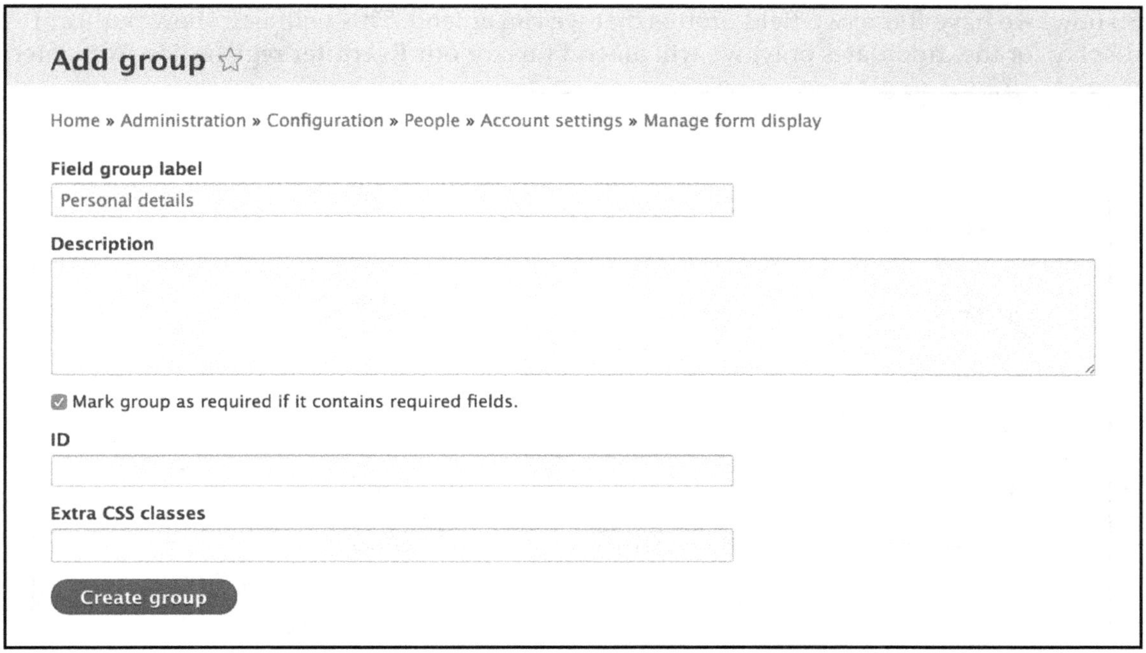

Add group ☆

Home » Administration » Configuration » People » Account settings » Manage form display

Field group label

Personal details

Description

☑ Mark group as required if it contains required fields.

ID

Extra CSS classes

Create group

Fig 1.13: Field group settings

In the preceding screenshot, the field group gives us additional fields we can use. We can add a description that appears in the field group element; making all the fields inside the field group required will override any fields we place into this field group regardless of whether they are not required. We can then add ID and css classes to the Fieldset that adds to the **Fieldset** element.

After clicking on **Create group**, we will be redirected to our form display page. Repeat this process and create a new field group with a widget of Fieldset. We will call this one **Job requirements**.

So now, we have these two field groups that we can amend. This will then show our form display for the candidates only; we will amend this for our **Recruiter** registration form later:

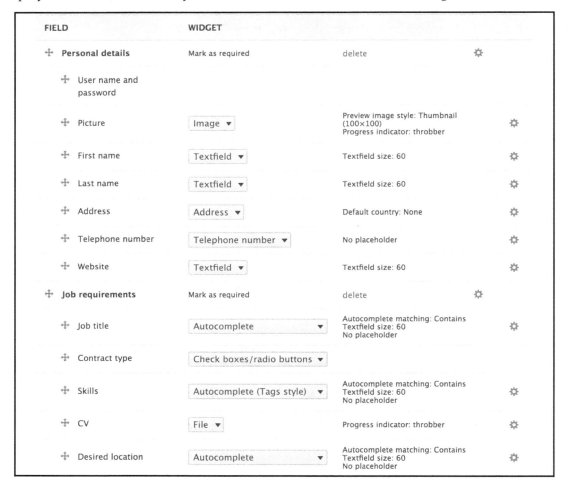

Fig 1.14: Candidate field layout

In the preceding figure, we can see that our fields are set out for **Candidate** view mode, which in turn will be our candidate user registration form. We will now sort the form layout for the **Recruiter** view mode. To do this, we will add a few more fields for the **Recruiter** registration from; however, we will switch a few fields about in our **Recruiter** view mode, so let's go back to **Manage fields.**

We will now add the following fields so that we can use them for our recruiter user profile and registration:

- **Company name**: Textfield
- **Recruiter description**: Text (formatted, long, with summary)
- **Logo**: Image

Once these are created, we will click on the **Recruiter** view mode and repeat the same process as we did for the **Candidate** view mode; however, we won't add any field groups for this:

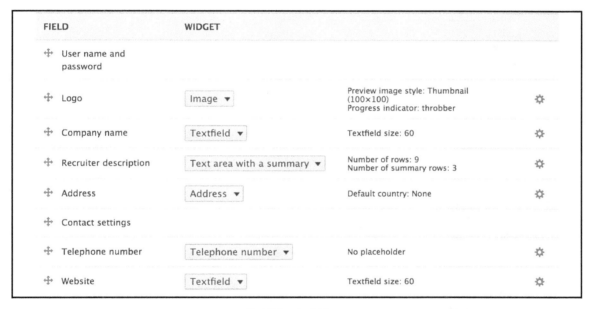

Fig 1.15: Recruiter field layout

Our **Recruiter** field layout should be as illustrated in the preceding screenshot.

Now that this is done, we need to separate our registration pages so that they are different for our user types. Going back to **Admin | Configuration** under **People**, click on **Registration types**. We want the user, after they have registered to be assigned a **Candidate** user role.

So, after this, we will see a page that has a table and has no entries; click on **+ Add Registration type.** The screen that will open next is as shown in this screenshot:

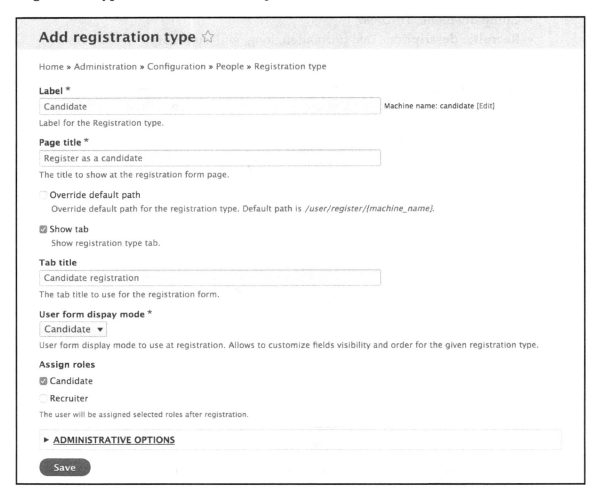

Fig 1.16: Add registration type

If we fill out our registration type as per the preceding screenshot, we can **Save** it, and do the same for **Recruiter** and change the **Candidate** aspects of the form to **Recruiter**.

Once this is done, let's open an incognito window and click on **Log in**. You will now see that we have five tabs on our **Log in** form:

Fig 1.17: Log in form

In the preceding screenshot, we have our tabs along with the **Log in** form; note that there is a **Create new account** option, which we will remove later.

If we click on **Candidate**, we will see the form we created, and the same for **Recruiter**. Let's create a user for each.

 Once we have done this, we will move on to creating a **Job** Content type that recruiters can create for the site.

After filling out our form for our candidate, we will see a message saying that an email has been sent. This email contains a one-time link that allows us to access Drupal's user admin interface:

Fig 1.18: People page with users

Once we are logged in and our account is active, go back to our browser window with the admin account logged in, and go to **People**, as we can see in the preceding screenshot.

Using Webform

Now that we have created our job vacancy content type, we will add the form to apply for that job; this will then appear for the recruiters. To do this, we will use another contrib module Webform (`https://drupal.org/project/webform`), and we will also add token (`https://drupal.org/project/token`).

Once this is added to our `composer` file, we will enable **Webform**, Webform UI, and Token.

We will then create our job application form; Webform allows us to create a form that can be attached to a node. This will allow us to easily relate the applications to the job, which will help us out with our **Recruiter** dashboard later on in this chapter.

To create a **Webform**, go to **Structure | Webforms**:

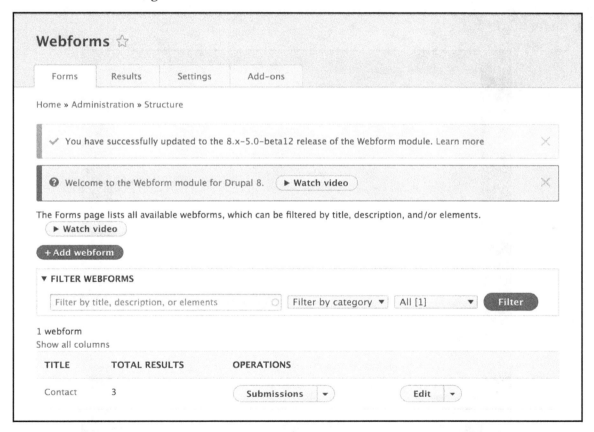

Fig 1.19: Webform admin

In the previous figure, we can see the admin interface used for Webform. As we want to create a new form specifically for applications, click on **+ Add webform**.

A popup then appears, which allows us to enter a title, description, and category. For this, we want to add **Application form** as our title and **Administrative description** as *A webform that allows candidate user roles to apply for a job.*

When we click on **Save**, we will be taken to our **Elements** page that will allow us to create our Webform. For this Webform, we want to just have a **Name** field, because the form will submit additional data. This includes the node it's referenced to and the user who submitted it; we can, of course, add other fields to this to make it more detailed, but we will keep ours simple.

To add fields, we click on **+ Add field**, and then we are shown a popup with a list of element types. For ours, we will pick a **Text field**. After doing this, we will see the settings form for this field:

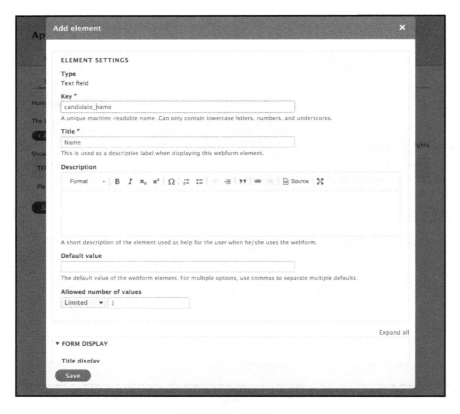

Fig 1.20: Webform field settings

As can be seen in the previous figure, the field has a lot of settings. For now, we will just add a **Name** field and click on **Save**. We will also add a **Fieldset** element to wrap around the field; this will just make it stand out more on the job vacancy page.

Once we have saved this, we can drag our **Name** field so that it is a child item of **Job application**:

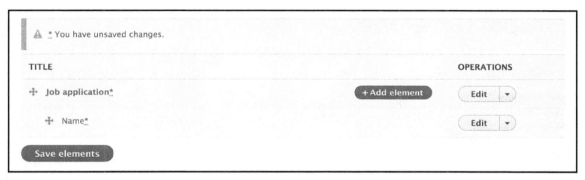

Fig 1.21: Form admin UI

In the preceding screenshot, we can see that our name is inside our **Job application Fieldset** item. This means that when we have it on our job vacancy, it will be displayed inside a nice Fieldset, which makes it stand out a bit more on the page.

Creating our job

Now that we have created our two user roles and set the registration process up, let's create some content for our jobs. For this, we will create a content type called **Job vacancy**.

As we have already covered how to do this, we will just cover what fields are needed for this, which will include the following fields:

- **Job title**: Textfield
- **Location**: Taxonomy
- **Closing date**: Date field
- **Job description:** Long text
- **Job category**: Taxonomy

We also have a new field reference type called Webform, with which we will attach our webform to our content type. So, create a new field type Webform and give it a name of **Apply for this job vacancy**.

From here, we will set our field to have a default value of **Application form**. Now, since we have saved this, we will hide it from our form display as we don't want our recruiter to see this. The form will display automatically on the job vacancy.

Using our recruiter user account, let's create a job vacancy and click on **Save**:

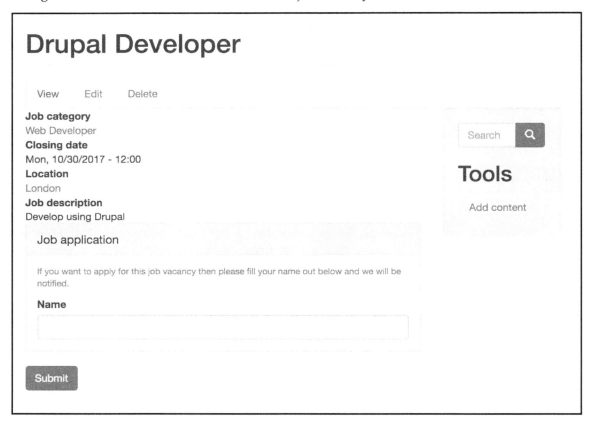

Drupal Developer

View   Edit   Delete

Job category
Web Developer
Closing date
Mon, 10/30/2017 - 12:00
Location
London
Job description
Develop using Drupal

Job application

If you want to apply for this job vacancy then please fill your name out below and we will be notified.

Name

Submit

Search 🔍

Tools

Add content

Fig 1.22: Job vacancy page

In the preceding screenshot, we can see that the form is now displaying. We don't want anonymous users to be able to create an application, so we need to modify it in a module.

Jobs module

To enhance our functionality on the site, we will need to create a module. To start off, it will simply hide the job application form from anonymous users. Start by creating our module called **jobs.**

jobs.info.yml

```
name: Jobs
description: Enhances job website functionality
core: 8.x
type: module
package: Recruitment site
```

Once we have done this, enable our `jobs` module. Now we can alter how our form works. To do this, we will use `hook_form_alter()`.

This allows us to override any form inside Drupal; it works based on the form ID. We can use a `switch()` statement to target multiple forms; however, we can also use `hook_form_FORM_ID_alter()`.

As the form ID uses our machine name, this is likely to be different; so for this, we will stick to `hook_form_alter()`.

What we want to achieve here is to allow the user to register if they are logged in, but if they are not, then we will show a message that says they must log in.

jobs.module

```php
<?php
/**
 * @file
 * Jobs enhancements.
 */

use Drupal\Core\Form\FormStateInterface;
use Drupal\Core\Url;
use Drupal\Core\Link;

/**
 * Implements hook_form_alter().
 */
function jobs_form_alter(&$form, FormStateInterface $form_state, $form_id)
{
  if ($form['#webform_id'] == 'application_form' &&
\Drupal::currentUser()->isAnonymous()) {
    unset($form['elements']['job_application']['candidate_name']);
    unset($form['actions']);

    $link = Link::fromTextAndUrl(t('login'), Url::fromRoute('user.login'),
array())->toString();
    $form['elements']['job_application']['#markup'] = t('You must be logged
in order to register, click here to @link', array('@link' => $link));
```

```
    }
  }
```

What we have done

The module we have just created allows us to do the following:

Based on the form itself being a web form, we get the `#webform_id` key, which allows us to target our `webform_id` that was created when the webform was created. We then do a check to see whether the current user is anonymous, which will then let us take out the **name** and **submit** button, which is what we do using `unset()`.

We then want to display our error message that prompts the user to log in; of course, we want to make it translatable so we use the `t()`. We then want to have the link go to our user login page; to do this, we create our link using `Link::fromTextandUrl()`, we then have two arguments we need inside this. We can get the specific route using our existing routes.

Now, if we do a cache rebuild and look at this page as an anonymous user, we will see our message; however, if we are logged in, then we will see the form. This type of functionality, no doubt, will appear in the contrib module, so this may need to be ignored.

Almost there

Now to recap, we have created the following so far:

- User roles (Candidate and Recruiter)
- Different registration forms
- Job vacancy content type
- Form to apply for a job vacancy
- Hide the from from anonymous users

We will now set our permissions so that Recruiters can create, edit, and delete their job vacancies:

Job vacancy. Create new content	☐	☐	☐	☑	☑
Job vacancy. Delete any content	☐	☐	☐	☐	☑
Job vacancy. Delete own content	☐	☐	☐	☑	☑
Job vacancy. Delete revisions Role requires permission to *view revisions* and *delete rights* for nodes in question, or *administer nodes*.	☐	☐	☐	☐	☑
Job vacancy. Edit any content	☐	☐	☐	☐	☑
Job vacancy. Edit own content	☐	☐	☐	☑	☑

Fig 1.23: Permissions set for recruiter

Set the permission as we have mentioned. What we have done is that only the Recruiter will be able to create a job vacancy, no other user role. So, we have all our functionality of applying for a job; we will now create our dashboard.

Dashboards for Recruiter

When our user logs in, we want to redirect them to /user/dashboard; this will show our jobs created or applied for based on who has applied. We will create this entire dashboard using views, and we'll have it as a page.

First, to do this, we need to redirect the user after they login; we will use hook_form_FORM_ID_alter() and a custom submit handler, as shown:

```
/**
 * Implements hook_form_FORM_ID_alter().
 */
function jobs_form_user_login_form_alter(&$form, FormState $form_state) {
  $form['#submit'][] = 'jobs_user_login_submit';
}

/**
 * Form submission handler for user_login_form().
 *
 * Redirects the user to the dashboard after logging in.
 */
function jobs_user_login_submit(&$form, FormState $form_state) {

  $request = \Drupal::service('request_stack')->getCurrentRequest();
  if (!$request->request->has('destination')) {
    $form_state->setRedirect('/user/dashboard');
```

```
        }
    }
```

The dashboard will show the jobs this user, who is our **Recruiter**, has created. With Webform, we can view the submissions on the form for this job. If we want to extend this functionality, then at the time of writing this the custom code will need to be written.

Now that we have our dashboard, our recruiters can create jobs and then view the jobs. Within our node, we can then view **Submissions** for that job.

Job search

To allow our jobs to be searched for on the site, let's create a new view called job search. For this view, we want to expose the job title, category, and location. To do this create a view with display type of page; we have already covered this earlier so this is a refresher on how to do it.

Then add whichever fields you want to display for this. Now this is done, add an exposed filter, you can then either leave the exposed form attached to the top, or show the form as a block.

Summary

We took a look at Composer and how Composer enhances development with Drupal and any development project. Then, we created multiple user role registrations that allow different information to be created by our user.

Upon registering, the user is then assigned a different user role, and, based on this, they can either create a job or apply for a job. This makes the process of creating or applying for a job a lot easier and easy to manage as to which user role can do it.

We created a Webform that is attached to each node, which then stores all submissions on the node so that the recruiter can view the job applications.

In the next chapter, we will look at how to create an event website; this will show an event with a schedule, and more.

5
List Properties with Drupal

If you run a property retail business, then you'll want to list properties you have on your portfolio online. In this chapter, we are going to create our own property company that will allow properties to be listed on the website. This will incorporate an ability to filter properties and manage them.

We will look at using as little custom code in this chapter as possible. We will be covering the following topics throughout the chapter:

- Creating a property content type
- Property display
- Using Display Suite
- Property search
- Administering our properties
- URL aliases

Getting prepared

Before we get started with our property listing website, let's do a clean Drupal installation.

Once we have done our new installation, let's remove the parts we don't specifically want on our website. Previously, we just left in the default configuration for our website; however, let's make our installation use just what we ideally want.

Cleaning up

First off, let's delete all our content types. To do this, go to **Admin** | **Structure** | **Content types** and select **Delete** on the content type; repeat this for the other content type.

Next, move to **Admin** | **Structure** | **Comment types** and repeat the same for our comment type. From here, go to **Admin** | **Extend** and then click on the **Uninstall** tab.

 Previous Drupal core versions allowed modules to be disabled; in Drupal 8, we need to uninstall them from the system configuration.

We need to select the following modules to uninstall:

- Comment
- Color

Now that we have done all of this for our property, we can start with creating our **Property** content type. We will also be using `field_group` for laying out our admin interface forms.

The fields we will need for our content type are as follows:

- Property name--Title
- Address--Address field
- Photos
- Floorplans
- Type of Property
- House
- Flat
- Rooms
- Bedrooms (number)
- Bathrooms (number)
- Reception rooms (number)
- Amenities (checkboxes)
- Garden
- Outbuilding
- Private parking
- Swimming pool
- Description (textarea)

- Price (field group)
- Amount (float)
- Monthly (boolean)

Now, we have added all the fields we need to make our form display look usable, we will amend our various field widgets. We will then click on **Manage form display**. The screen that comes next is as follows:

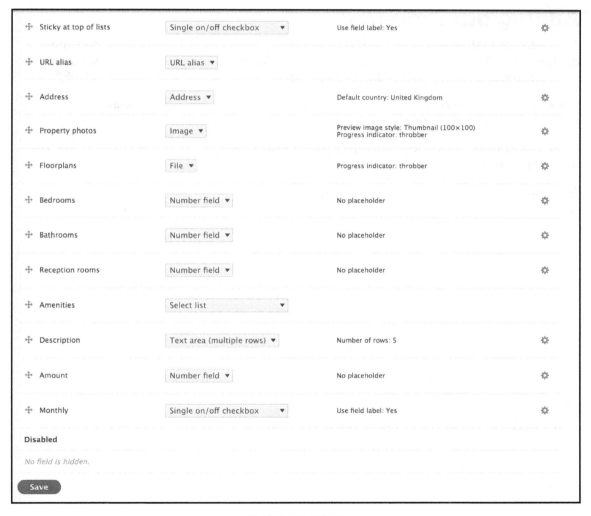

Fig 1.0: Manage form display

We will then change **Amenities** from the **Select** list to **Checkboxes/radio buttons**. This allows us to change the output of what our user will see. It also means we could write a widget that could have a different approach to multiselect.

Now that this is done, we will create our first property. This will allow us to have the basic look for our **Property** page. From this, we will then change the look of our **Property** pages.

Adding our Property

To create our first property as we have previously created content, we will go to **Admin | content**. From here, we will click **+ Add content**. However, as we only have one content type, Drupal knows that this is the type of content you want to enter. Pretty cool, eh?

We will now see our content page. As per the previous content types, it is structured in the same way. We can, however, change this layout if we so wished.

Let's create our first property. Fill out some dummy content and, once we have done this, we will move on.

For now, we won't upload any images or files. This is to keep what we are doing clean and simple.

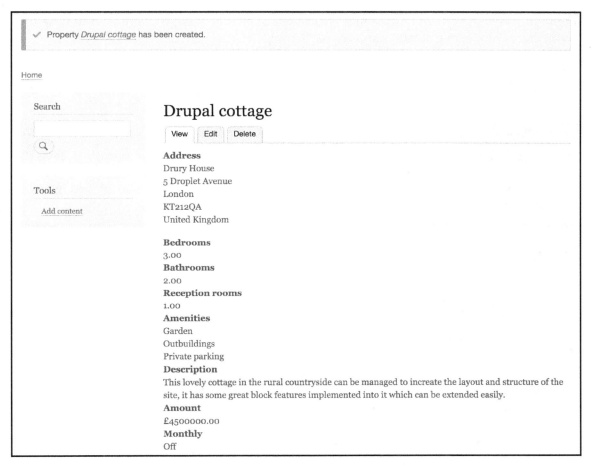

Great! So, we now have our first property created! It's looking a bit plain.

Enhancing our content

So, we have just created our basic look for the **Property** page. It's not that great and, as a website builder for this bit, we can leverage the contrib modules available to Drupal to make the layout more flexible.

There are a few options in Drupal that we can use to change this. At the time of writing this book, there were experimental modules for layouts in the core.

What we will look at are two very popular contrib modules that have similar functionality. These two approaches are **Display Suite** and **Panels**.

Display Suite

So, what Display Suite allows us to do is use a layout in a similar way to our **Block layout** is create sections for the template. This can allow someone with no real developer skills the ability to control the layout of the content. To control how our content is displayed, go to **Admin | Structure | Displays**.

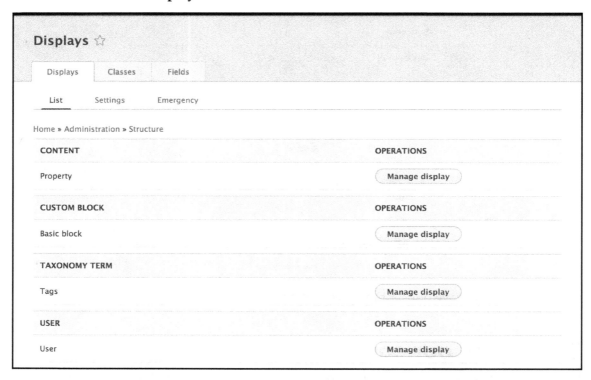

Fig 1.3: Display suite layout

We can easily access our content display from this page. We can also access our content display by going to **Manage display** in our content type, but this interface is a quick and easy way to manage our content being displayed. Once on this page, we can change our layout.

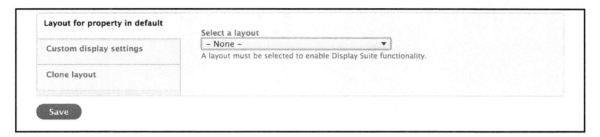

Fig 1.4: Layout settings

In *Fig 1.4*, we can see the options to set the layout for our content in vertical tabs and ensure our **Custom display settings** is also a tab. We have some preset layouts added to the display options.

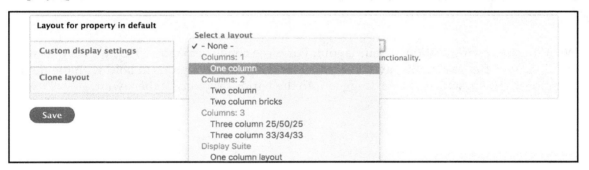

Fig 1.5: Layout options on Manage Display

For our property display, we will show ours in two columns, so select **Two column layout**.

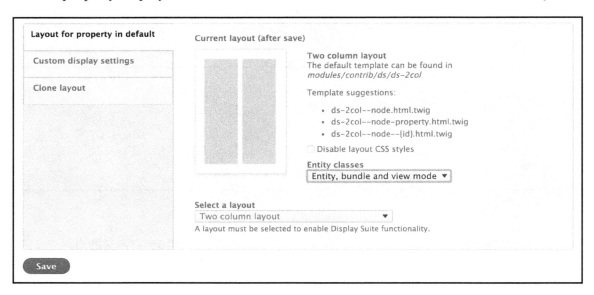

Fig 1.6: Settings for content layout

We now have configuration for our layout. For these changes to take effect, we need to save our display. After saving the layout settings, we will see two regions in bold with the fields underneath them, which can be dragged into the various regions of the layout.

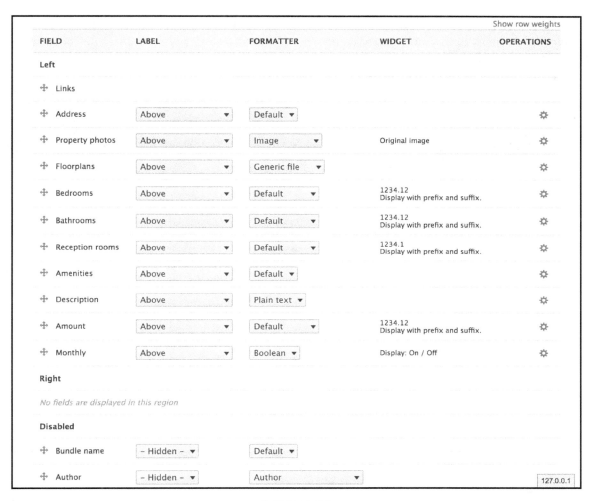

Fig 1.7: Layout admin

Now that we have our layout set out, drag some fields into each column, and then click **Save**. Then, go back to your property and you will see how simple our layout has become. We have not had to do any styling.

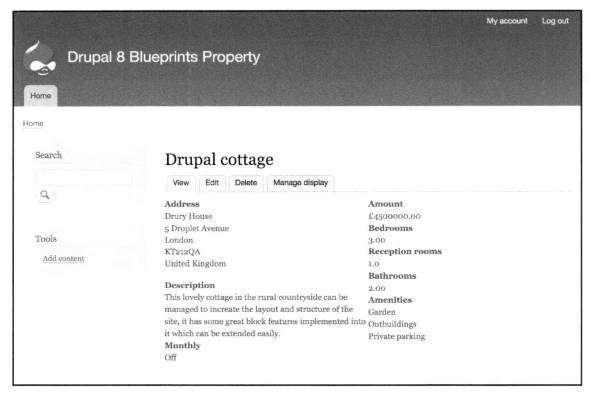

Fig 1.8: Property page with columns

So, now that we have a starting place for our **Property**, let's tidy it up a bit more and move over to using our bootstrap theme. As with any field widget, we can change the settings on them to suit our needs, and if there isn't a widget there, we can make our own.

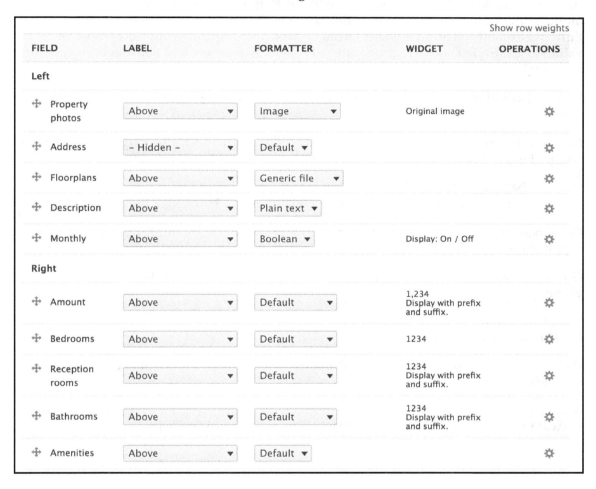

Fig 1.9: Layout with fields widget amended

Now, as per the preceding screenshot, we can see that our fields are split into our layout that we set up using the default layout options.

As we have done the basics on this, let's edit our **Property photos** so that we can show multiple images. Go back to **Manage fields** and look for **Property photos** and then click **Edit**. Once on this page, go to **Field settings**. We will change the **Allowed number of values** to **Unlimited**, as we're promoting a Property. So, we want to allow as many photos as possible.

Moving back to our Property, let's add some photos. We will use photos from (`https://pixabay.com`) for this.

Now that we have added our photos, let's add a slideshow to our **Property** page. To do this, we will be using Flex Slider (`https://www.drupal.org/project/flexslider`).

Once we have downloaded Flex Slider using the Composer `composer require drupal/flexslider`, we will then enable **FlexSlider** and **FlexSlider Views Style**.

Once these are enabled, then what we will do is create a view for our **Property photos**, so now head over to **Views** and create our view.

Give your view a name like **Property photos** and a description of **Slideshow for current property**.

For this to work, our views block will take an argument based off the current node we are on. This way, we only have to create the view once.

We want to show **Content** of the type **Property**. Then, check **Create a block** and click **Save and edit**.

Now, we can see our configuration for our view. As we are using the **FlexSlider** module, we want to change the Format to use **FlexSlider**, so click on **FlexSlider**.

Fig 1.10: View Format

In the preceding screenshot, we can see the options we have. As we add modules that have plugins for views, more will appear here for us to select.

Once we have selected **FlexSlider** and clicked **Apply**, we can see some more options for our Format style.

What we can see for the **FlexSlider** options are as follows:

- **Option set**: This allows us to choose how our **FlexSlider** image gallery is displayed. There are a lot of settings for this. We can create multiple option sets.
- **Caption field**: This will take a value from a field that will appear in our view row.
- **Element ID**: This allows us to uniquely identify our **FlexSlider** on a page.

We will keep our **Option** set as **Default**, but we will configure this bit later on to display how we want. For **Caption Field**, we will leave it as **None** for now. Now that this is done, click **Apply**.

So, all we will see is our property name. This is because the only field we have added is our node title. Let's change this and add our actual **Property photo**. Remove the **Title** field by clicking on it and clicking **Remove**. Next, click on **Add** and then select **Property photos** from our fields list and click **Add and configure fields**.

From here, we will now configure our photos for the **FlexSlider**. Our **FlexSlider** will take the field and implement into the `FlexSlider javascript` plugin.

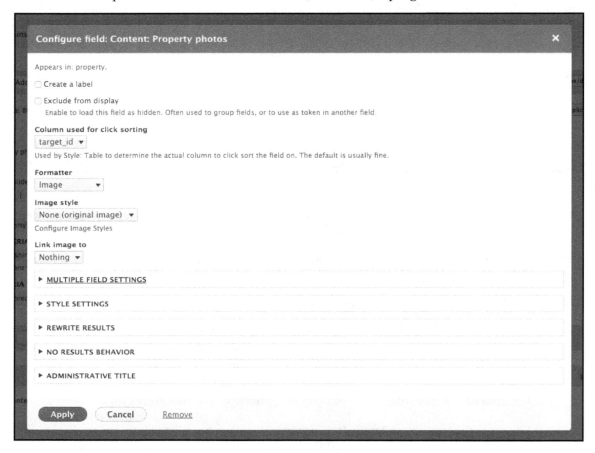

Fig 1.11: Field settings

In the preceding screenshot, we have our common field settings dialog. As we want to show our main image to be big, we will select an image style of **Large**. You may notice there are a few other image styles listed there. We can, of course, add more image styles by clicking **Configure Image Styles**.

Image styles are a global asset and can be used anywhere we have images. They define certain rules for how an image is rendered.

As our image field has multiple values, we want to show these on separate rows. In order to do this, click **Multiple Field Settings** and uncheck **Display all values in the same row**; you will notice that once you do this, the options disappear, as we don't need to configure any of this.

After this, click **Apply**. In our preview, we can see our image in a slideshow. The basics for this is now done, but we will return to this to improve the slideshow. But currently, we just have a block. Now, we could, of course, just go to **Block layout** and add our block that way, but we can only add it to our regions that we have configured. If we have a funky layout for our content already, then this will defeat the point of this.

We will now add a **Display Suite** field that will allow us to add our view to our content display for any content.

Adding custom fields to our display

Display suite has a lot of extra goodness that we are going to look at now. As we want to add our new property photos block into our content, we need to create a new field. In order to do this, we need to add some configuration to our **Displays**.

Go to **Admin | Structure**. Once on this page, look for **Display Suite** and click it.

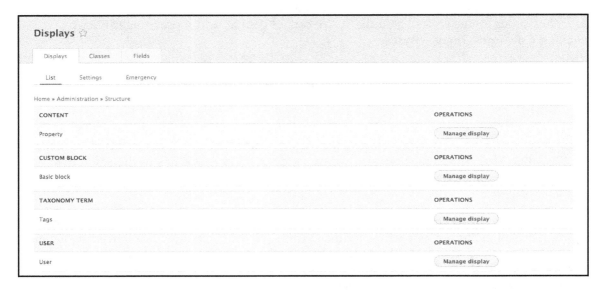

Fig 1.12: Display Suite displays configuration

We can see in *Fig 1.12* that all our entity types can have their very own display controlled using **Display Suite**. There are three main sections in **Display Suite**:

- **Displays List**: This shows all the current displays available in Drupal and allows them to be configured
- **Settings**: This allows us to configure various settings that will affect all the fields in Drupal used with **Display Suite**
- **Emergency**: If there are any issues with the field, then they can be disabled from that display while you fix it (this is handy because previously the website would break)
- **Classes**: From here, we can add additional classes to our regions. We can define them here and use them on our **Manage display** screens
- **Fields**: We can create additional fields here that will allow us to use within our content throughout the website

Now, we have an understanding of how the settings in **Display Suite** work. We will create our new field that we want to expose to our **Displays**. Go to the **Fields** tab and, from here, click **+ Add a block field**. What this will do is allow us to take any block we have created (just like our property photos block) and expose as a field.

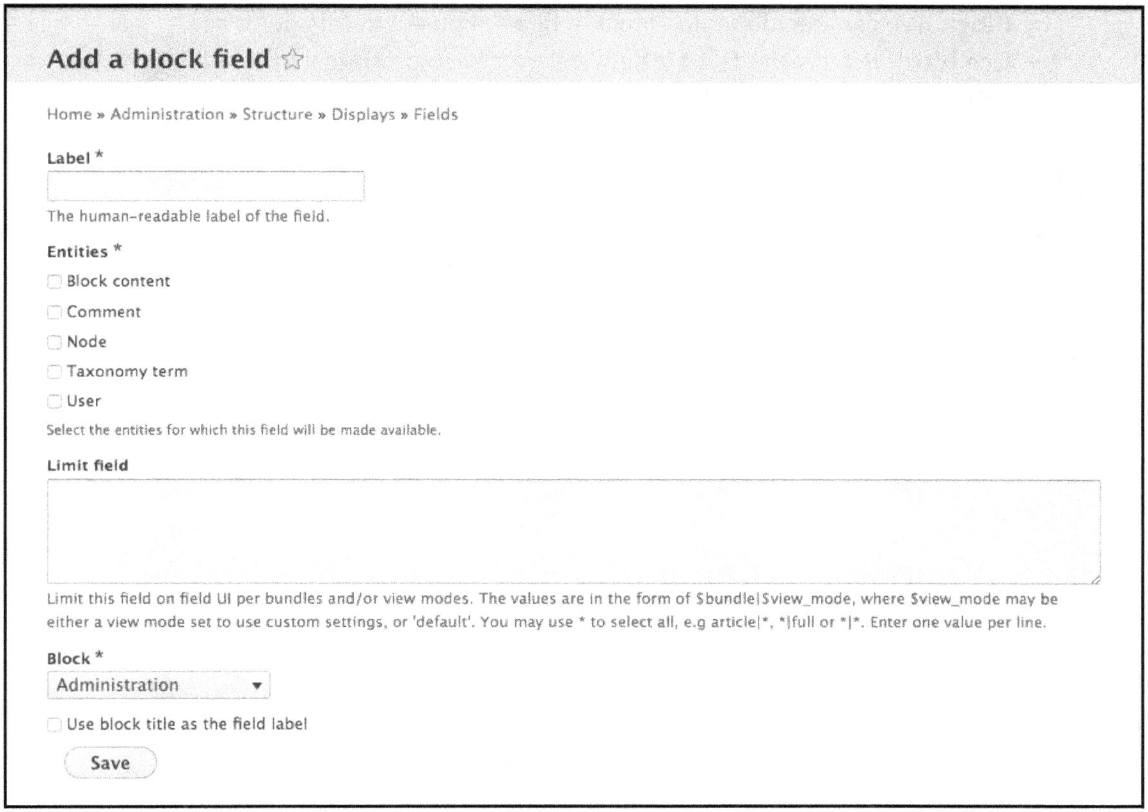

Add a block field ☆

Home » Administration » Structure » Displays » Fields

Label *

The human-readable label of the field.

Entities *

☐ Block content

☐ Comment

☐ Node

☐ Taxonomy term

☐ User

Select the entities for which this field will be made available.

Limit field

Limit this field on field UI per bundles and/or view modes. The values are in the form of $bundle|$view_mode, where $view_mode may be either a view mode set to use custom settings, or 'default'. You may use * to select all, e.g article|*, *|full or *|*. Enter one value per line.

Block *

Administration ▾

☐ Use block title as the field label

(Save)

Fig 1.13: Block field settings

In *Fig 1.13*, we can see we have our configuration:

- **Label**: This is our unique name for this field that will be shown under our Field column in our **Manage display** for our entity. This will also create a machine name, which is unique for this field.
- **Entities**: This is great because we can decide to just expose this field on certain entity types.
- **Limit field**: If we decide that we only want this field on a certain bundle and view mode, then this will let us list them here.

- **Block**: We can decide which block will be exposed to this field.
- **Use block title as the field label**: This can keep our block and field consistent, so there's no confusion and multiple names given.

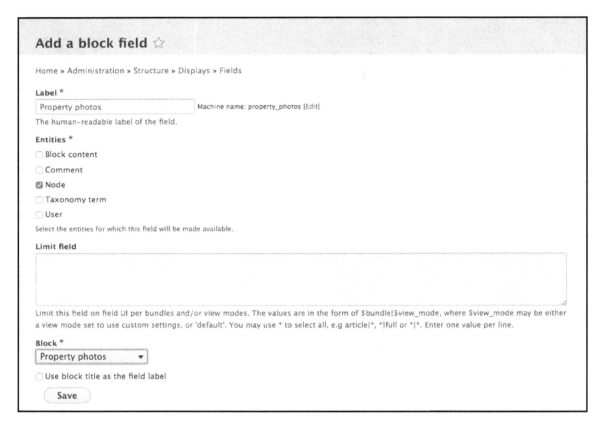

Fig 1.14: Block field settings

In *Fig 1.14*, all our fields settings are done for how we need it, so click **Save** and we will then be asked how many **Items per block** we want; just save this as the default.

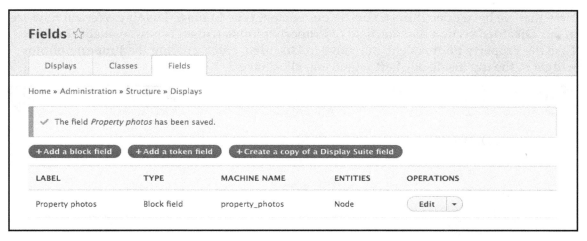

Fig 1.15: Newly created custom field

Now that we have created our new field, we can see it in the **Fields** listing page. This now means it's available to our content type.

Let's add this to our **Property** display, so go to the content type and then **Manage Display**.

You can also go back to the entity type **Manage Display** by clicking the **Displays** tab when inside the **Display Suite** configuration.

Once we are back in our **Displays**, if we scroll down under **Disabled**, we will see our new field. We will see, however, that there are two fields with the label of **Property photos**. This is going to be really confusing later on, let's change this now. Go back to **Display Suite** Configuration **Admin | Structure | Display Suite** and then to the **Fields** tab and click **Edit** on the **Property photos** row. Change the label to **Property photos widget**.

As the machine name has already been created, it won't be amended; only the human-readable label will change.

Now that we have done this, go back to our content type **Manage Display**. We will now see in our **Disabled** section that our field of **Property photos widget** is now available to use. Take the **Property photos** field and move to **Disabled**, and then drag the **Property photos widget** to the top inside our **Left** region and click **Save**.

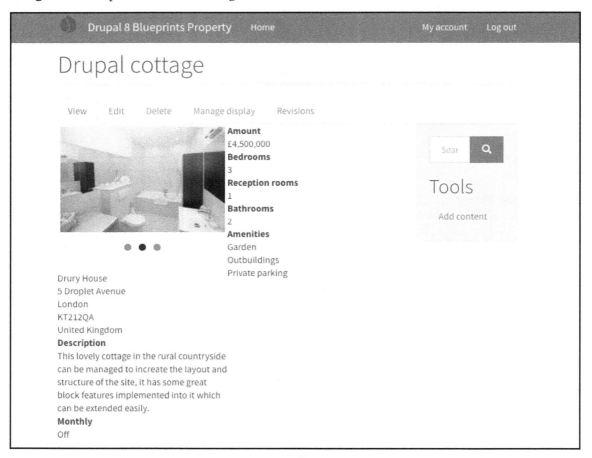

Fig 1.16: Property page with photos

We now have our photo slideshow in place. But if we were to add another property, then all of our photos for all our properties would be on show. So, what we are going to do is add an argument or known to us in views as a contextual filter. We have covered this previously, but we will cover it again as we need to take a different argument this time.

Fig 1.17: Editing content blocks

If we want to edit content as a user with certain permissions, we can hover over the block of content we want to edit. In Drupal 8, we can do a quick edit for block and node content. But in our case, for the view, we want to quickly make our changes to it, save it, and return back to where we are currently.

If we click on the pencil icon that appears on top of our image, then an **Edit view** dropdown will appear. By clicking this, we will be taken to our configuration page for that view.

Once we ware on our view configuration display page on the right-hand side column at the top under **Contextual Filters**, click **Add** as before and the fields popup will appear, as we want to take the ID as our argument and match it up to our node ID the content is related to.

After selecting **Content: ID**, ensure that the **Provide default value** is selected, change **Type** to be **Content ID from URL**, and click **Apply**, as we have no argument for our contextual filters. Then, nothing will be shown. However, change the argument to 1 and click **Update preview** and we can then see our images. Now, click **Save** and we will be returned to the previous page we were on. But how does Drupal know where to go I hear you ask?

Well in the URL `admin/structure/views/view/property_photos/edit/block_1?destination=node/1`, we can see our path to our view. Then, from there, we have an argument that Drupal uses `?destination=node/1`. This is basically saying, after I've completed my task on this page, take me back to where I was.

Of course, if we don't want to go back there, we can just remove it from the path. Now, we go back to our property display.

Property search

Now that we have our first property created, we want our users to be able to search for properties on the website. To do this, we are going to remove the search field that is being used and add a form to the right-hand side region. Of course, you can place the search field anywhere you like.

Generate dummy content

Working with one node doesn't really give a good feel to how the website would behave with multiple properties. Instead of making up a whole bunch of fake properties and finding pictures, all we care about for now-while we develop the website-is content. Remember content is the king.

To do this, we have a fantastic module that comes with **Devel**. It's called **Devel Generate**.

As we already have Devel enabled, we don't need to download anything additional. We just need to enable it.

Once the module is enabled, do a cache rebuild. Then head to **Admin | Configuration**:

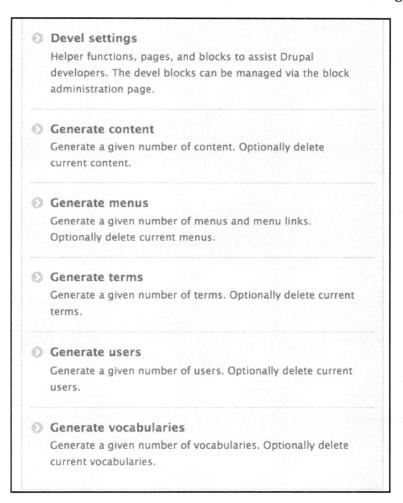

Devel settings

Helper functions, pages, and blocks to assist Drupal developers. The devel blocks can be managed via the block administration page.

Generate content

Generate a given number of content. Optionally delete current content.

Generate menus

Generate a given number of menus and menu links. Optionally delete current menus.

Generate terms

Generate a given number of terms. Optionally delete current terms.

Generate users

Generate a given number of users. Optionally delete current users.

Generate vocabularies

Generate a given number of vocabularies. Optionally delete current vocabularies.

Fig 1.18: Devel Generate options

In *Fig 1.18*, we can see all of our Devel module options. There are five types of entities that can be generated here. As we want to generate a multiple amount of property nodes, click on **Generate content**.

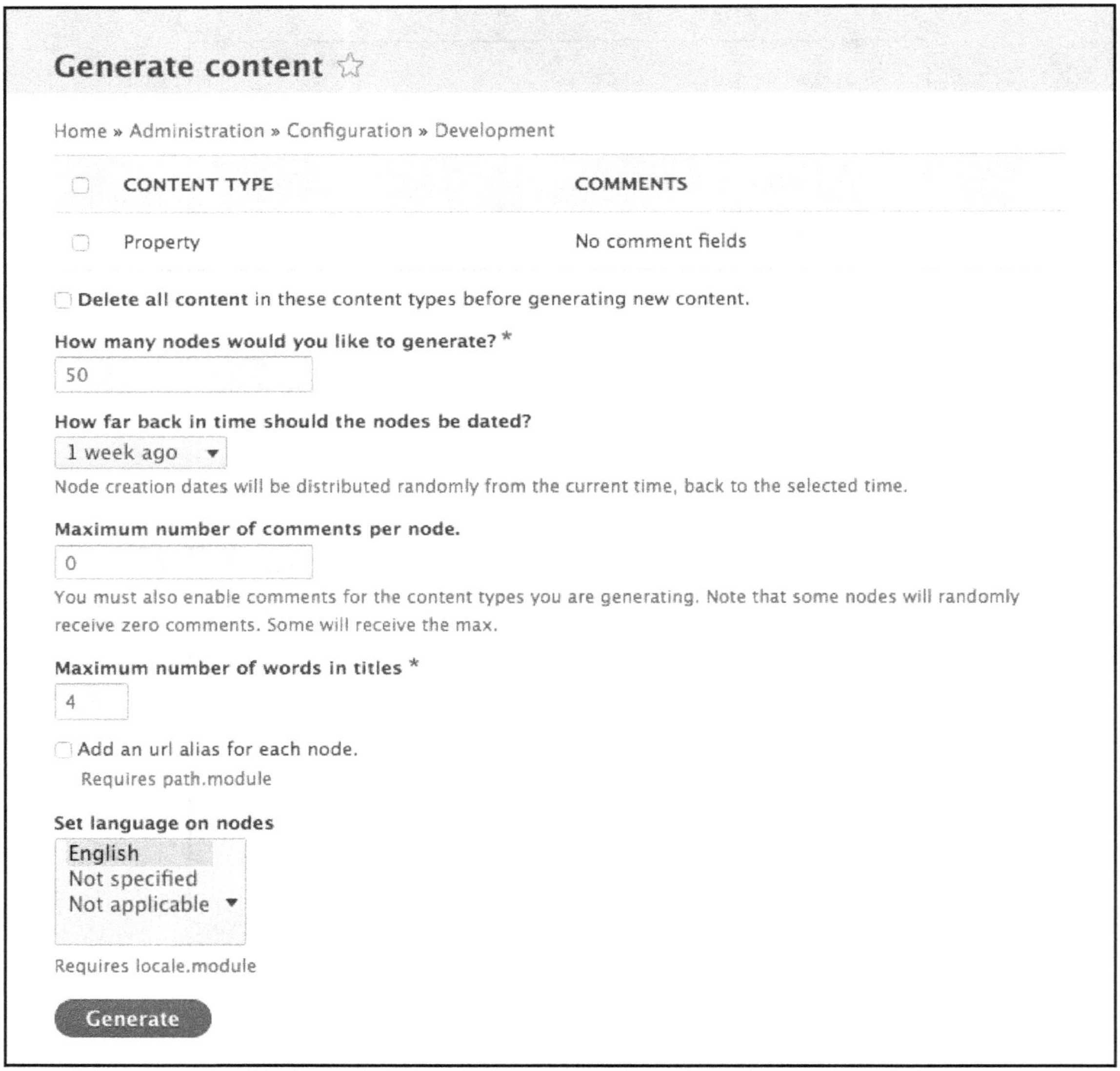

Generate content ☆

Home » Administration » Configuration » Development

☐	CONTENT TYPE	COMMENTS
☐	Property	No comment fields

☐ **Delete all content** in these content types before generating new content.

How many nodes would you like to generate? *

```
50
```

How far back in time should the nodes be dated?

```
1 week ago   ▼
```

Node creation dates will be distributed randomly from the current time, back to the selected time.

Maximum number of comments per node.

```
0
```

You must also enable comments for the content types you are generating. Note that some nodes will randomly receive zero comments. Some will receive the max.

Maximum number of words in titles *

```
4
```

☐ Add an url alias for each node.
  Requires path.module

Set language on nodes

```
English
Not specified
Not applicable   ▼
```

Requires locale.module

[Generate]

Fig 1.19: Generate content

In *Fig 1.19*, we can see all our settings for generating our content. When we have multiple content types, we will see in the table multiple rows.

We can then decide the following:

- How many nodes we want to generate
- How far back should the node created date be
- How many comments should the nodes have (if the content type has comments enabled)
- How many words should the title be
- Should a URL path be generated instead of `node/{nid}`
- What languages should the node be created in (if multiple languages are enabled)
- Now that we have filled all our requirements out, and for now, set the number of nodes to `10`, and clicked **Generate**, we will have `10` properties generated for us to continue to build our website

The only issue doing generate is it will do exactly that and generate everything random based off the type of field, so you may have to edit some of the nodes.

As we now have our dummy content created, let's go and create our property search.

Property search

To do this, we will use views again. So, let's go and create a new view. Let's call our view **Property search** and we want to show **Content** of the type **Property**. Then, we want to have this as our **Property** page, so check **Create a page** and give it a title of **Property search** and a path of `/properties`.

Now, set **Format** to **Grid** and then leave our **Style options** as they are and click **Apply**.

Click on **Content**. What you will now notice is we have **Display Suite: Content**. This allows us to use **Display Suite** layouts that we have set up, and we can use a specific view mode. So, select this one and click **Apply**. We will then be shown **Row style options** and a dropdown with our **View mode**. Beneath that, we have specific settings for the **Display Suite**. Let's just keep these as the default and click **Apply**.

If you look down, you can see our preview is now showing our **Property title** and a **Read more** link. When we visit this property listing, we will be able to click this link and it will take us directly to the property.

Exposed filters as a block

Inside our view, we have the option to expose our search filter by default. This will then generate a form that will appear at the top of our view. However, if we decided we want to have our search form on every page, then we need to convert the form to a block.

Let's start by exposing our locality part for our address field we created, so click **Add**, search for **locality**, and select that row. Repeat the same for administrative_area; again, repeat this and select country_code for our website. We will have properties in United Kingdom, but you can have yours wherever you want, and finally, add postal_code and click **Add and configure filter criteria**.

Now that's done, you will see the settings for our first filter, which is for country code. Select the option to be **United Kingdom** and click **Apply**. Change the label to say **Town/City**, select **The value of an exposed filter** and then **Expose this filter to visitors, to allow them to change it**, and click **Apply**.

Next onto **locality** and select the checkbox for **Expose this filter to visitors, to allow them to change it**. When you do this, you will notice that more options appear. Set the label as **County** and click **Apply and continue**. Finally, select **Expose this filter to visitors, to allow them to change it**, change the label to **Postcode** and the operator to **Contains**, and click **Apply**.

Now that this is done, we want to separate our property filter from the form and place on the left-hand side. To do this, on the right-hand side, go to **Exposed form** and, where it says **Exposed form in block**, click on **No** and then change it to **Yes**. This will now allow our **Exposed form** to appear as a block and, upon submitting from it, it will post the data to the page the view is rendered on, which in our case is /property-search. Once this is done, click **Save**. When we now go to /property-search, we can see our property on display. However, we cannot see our **Exposed form**. In order to add this form, we need to go to **Admin | Structure | Block layout** and move down to **Primary**. Here, we can now add our property search form. We want to have it appear on every page; click **Place block** and then look for a label that says **Exposed form** and then the view name and display name in it. In this case, it is **Exposed form: property_search-page_1** and click **Place block**.

Uncheck **Display title** and click **Save block** and then **Save blocks**. Now, we will have our property search the form on every page, and when we search for a property, we will be redirected to the listing page with our search results. If we enter part of our **Postcode** and click **Apply**, we will see our search results change. But now that we have this, let's add a price filter and some amenities to our form.

So, go back into the **View** and, under filter, click **Add**. Then, add **Amenities, Amount, Bathrooms**, and **Bedrooms**. For each, we want to **Expose this filter to visitors, to allow them to change it** and change the label for each. As we want to add multiple amenities, select **Allow multiple selections**. Then, for **Amount**, we want to have an amount that is less than or equal.

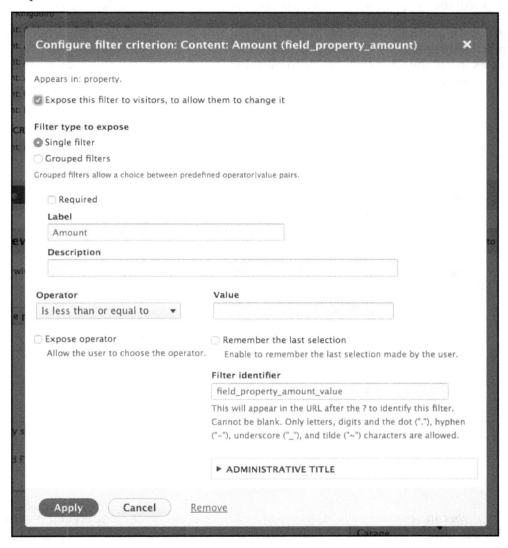

Fig 1.20: Property value

In *Fig 1.20*, we have the settings for our property amount. Once this is done, we will then need to convert our **Exposed form** to use the contrib module **Better Exposed Filters** (`https://drupal.org/project/better_exposed_filters`).

After this is done, go to the right column and look for **Exposed form style** and click on this. A popup will then appear with a choice of form styles, and select **Better Exposed Filters**.

Next, there are some options to set for the form style. These include changing the **Submit** button text, whether or not to have a reset button, show sort type. What we will change is **Amenities** to use the **Checkboxes/Radio buttons**. This give the user a little bit more control over their options.

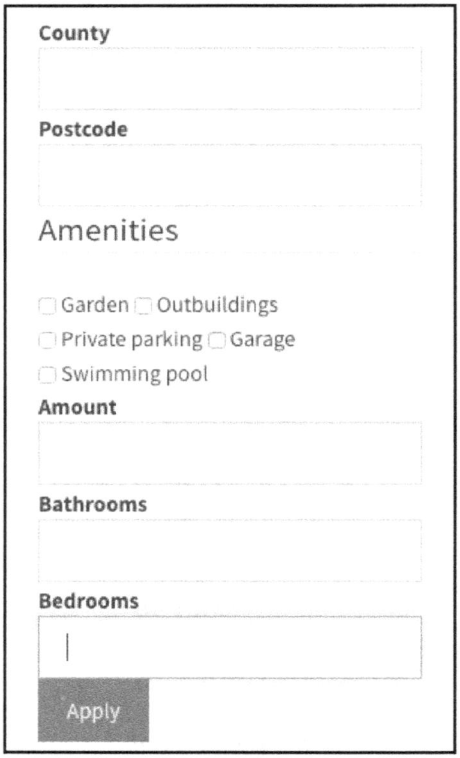

Fig 1.21: Property exposed filter

In *Fig 1.21*, we can see our newly created form. Obviously, there is some styling that needs to be done to this, but this form will now filter results and then, upon submitting the form, will show the results on our `/property-search`.

Now that we have done this, we can create the two other views we need, one that shows four random other properties and another that shows. Go back to the **View** and click **+ Add**; then, select **Block**. Once this is done, we need to remove all the fields and filters. Once we have done this, we will move to the middle column, click on **Use pager**, and select **Display a specified number of items**.

Remember to change the **For** dropdown to only say **This block (override)**; otherwise, we will make the changes to all the view displays.

Once we select this and click **Apply (this display)**, we will be taken to another set of options.

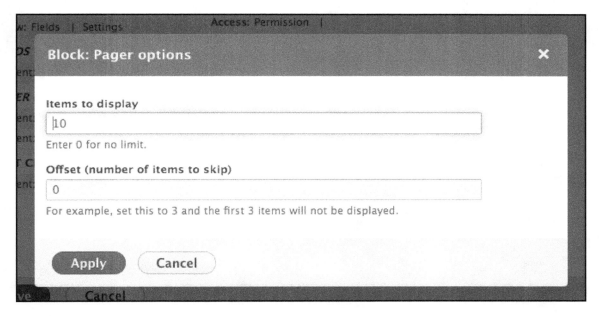

Fig 1.22: Pager options

In *Fig 1.22*, we can see our options for how many items will be displayed. We can also decide to skip the first set of items, so we don't just show the first four items. Then, once this is done, we can save our block and attach to our page. What we want to do is attach it only to the **Property** pages. To do this, we need to go to **Admin I Structure I Block Layout**.

Go to the content region, click **Place block** and then **+ Add custom block**, and select the block from the list. Select **Content types** to be **Property** and then click **Save block**.

Administer our properties

Now that we have properties set up, let's make a nice interface for our administrators to use.

Once again, we will be using views to do this.

So, create a new view called **Property management**. However, for the first time, we will be using admin in our path. Let this path be `admin/property-management`; this doesn't actually do anything. We will set the access permissions for this page shortly.

Once we have set our path for this page, we will set the **Displays** format to **Table** and click **Save and edit**.

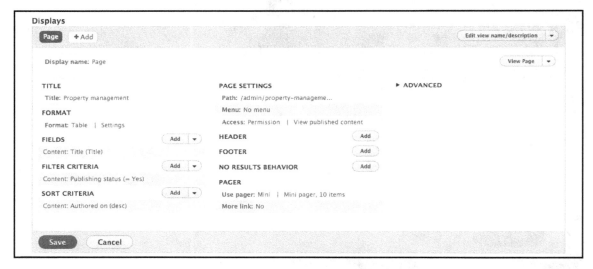

Fig 1.23: Views UI

Inside the views UI, we can see in the center column, there is a setting called **Access**. What this allows us to do is tell Drupal what rules must be met in order for this page to be accessible.

There are two types of access rules for a **View** page display:

1. We can decide if we want to use a permission that either already that exists or create our own.
2. We can use a User role.

For this, we will use a **User role** and select **Administrator**. Of course, we can come back later on and add additional roles after we have created them.

Great! So, now we are starting to see our administration page for our **Properties**. By default, as we only have **Property** content type content published, we will just see this. However, later on, if we add more content types and publish content, we will see these too, though being slightly confusing for a properly administration page. Let's filter down our content type to be specifically for **Property**.

Add a content type from the filter criteria and select **Property** content type and click **Apply**. Nothing will change in our **Preview**, but again, this is because we don't have any other content.

Now, we need to add the exposed filters for our properties. Add **Amenities** and **Monthly**, and expose both. Once this is done, we will change **Exposed form style** to **Better Exposed Filters**. This time, however, we will check **Autosubmit** (this allows the form to resubmit and reload the content without having to need the page to reload) and **Hide submit button**.

We will set our fields to be **Checkboxes/Radio Buttons**; after this, click **Apply**. If you change the filter values, then inside **Views**, you will notice that nothing changes. This is because Drupal restricts the Ajax JS loading to keep it less resource-intensive, especially for larger requests.

If, however, you save the view and go directly to the path, you will see the page loads, and if you change the filter values, then the content will update. Although this is a nice feature to have on larger scale websites, this is not advisable, as it is very resource-intensive and can cause the page to timeout.

From this page, we can go back into our view and add additional filters or columns of data to appear on this page.

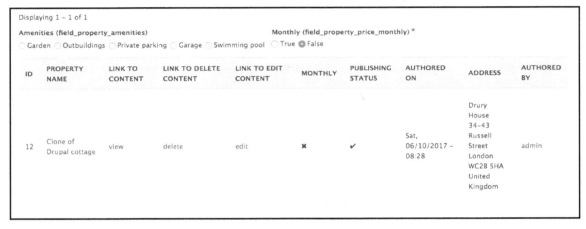

Fig 1.24: Additional fields added

Inside *Fig 1.24*, we can see additional fields available to the row of data that have been added, and our results are only showing monthly properties. This now allows us to administer our properties easier and filter them.

SEO-friendly paths

With Drupal, we can create our own paths for our content. However, this can become laborious and inconsistent. In order to keep consistency, we will use the contrib module **Pathauto** (https://drupal.org/project/pathauto). What this allows us to do is generate paths based off certain rules using tokens and means we can perform bulk tasks for this with ease. So, let's download this module. You will notice we will also need **ctools** (https://drupal.org/project/ctools) and **token** (https://drupal.org/project/token) for this.

Once this is done, go to **Admin | Configuration** and, under **Search and metadata**, click **URL aliases**. Then, from here, click on the tab **Patterns**. We will now create a pattern for our property content type.

We can have multiple patterns for each entity type and we can filter this down even more.

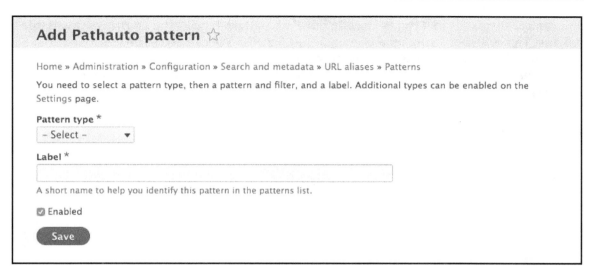

Click **+ Add Pathauto pattern**. In *Fig 1.25*, we can see the settings form for our pattern. Select **Pattern type** as **Content** and then a **Path pattern**.

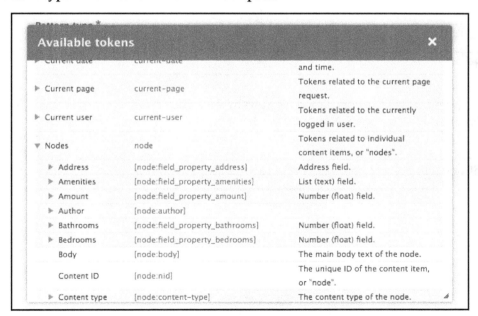

Fig 1.26: Available tokens

We can access tokens that can be used in our **Path pattern** by clicking on **Browse available tokens**. This will then bring up a popup, as per *Fig 1.26*. We can access tokens to use that can also be based off fields created in this content type. As we want to use the property title, we will use the token [node:title]. This will also strip any spaces and make the path lowercase with – in between words.

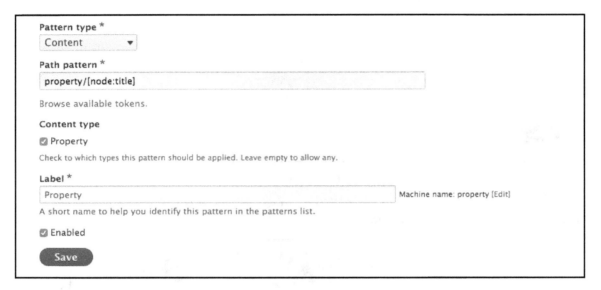

Fig 1.27: Completed pattern for property content type

In *Fig 1.27*, we can see the completed form. When we click **Save**, we will be taken back to the **Pattern type** listing page. Now that we have saved this pattern, we can run a bulk update for all our paths by clicking on the **Bulk generate** tab and then selecting which entity type and then the type of URL aliases to generate. Then, upon clicking **Update**, all these entities will be updated based off them having a pattern.

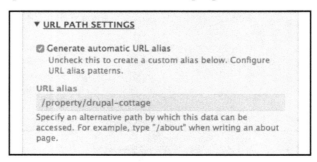

Fig 1.28: URL Path settings

If we go back to our first property and edit it, we will now see under **URL PATH SETTINGS** that, by default, the field is disabled and the path is generated.

Summary

From this chapter, we have learned how to harness the power of the core and contrib modules to build our website's functionality.

We have looked at Display Suite and how a simple website layout can be built as well as adding new fields and views into our page, adding a view for our property photos using a contrib module, and showing the properties photos based off a contextual filter.

We also spoke of using views to run the database queries, which in turn allows us to filter our results based off criteria and then expose the form so our users can use the form and change the search results in our view and implementing enhancements for the views filters.

Now in the next chapter we will move onto build an event website using mostly Drupal 8.x core very similar to how most Drupalcon and Drupalcamp event websites are built, this is also reflective of my event distribution called Cream (`https://drupal.org/projcet/cream`).

6
Express Your Event with Drupal

This is becoming more and more a request from clients to have an event website, where you can manage and run your event all using a website.

This chapter is largely based off the Cream distribution (`https://drupal.org/project/cream`) and a simpler approach to how it was built. Cream is one of the distributions I maintain. In fact, it runs off the second biggest Drupalcamp in the world. As it stated at the beginning, I'm one of the organisers of Drupalcamp London and have been so since 2013.

What we found was important in an event is the following:

- Session submissions
- Session feedback (using Disqus)
- Session management
- Schedules
- Sponsor signup and management
- Social media integration (twitter, facebook)
- Location of the venue
- Selling tickets (we'll use Drupal Commerce for this)

Getting started

So, as per our previous chapters, we will use a clean Drupal install.

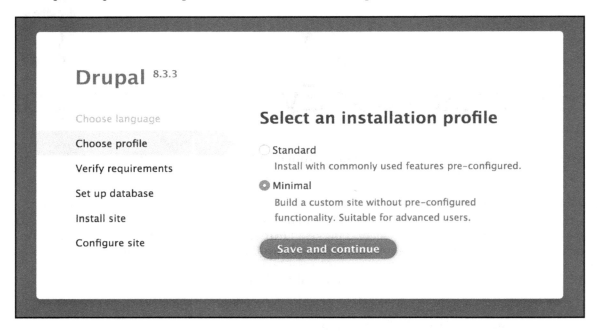

This time, let's install it using **Minimal** installation profile, and build up what we want from a lighter setup.

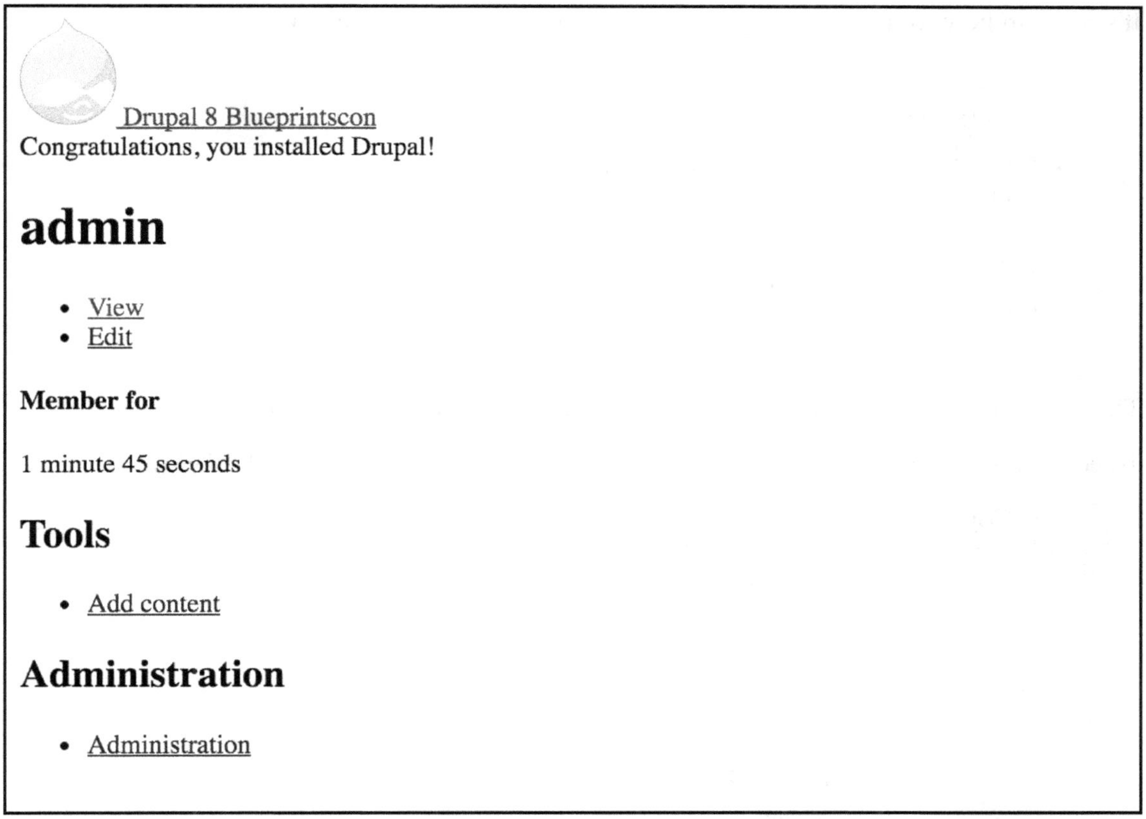

Drupal 8 Blueprintscon

Congratulations, you installed Drupal!

admin

- View
- Edit

Member for

1 minute 45 seconds

Tools

- Add content

Administration

- Administration

Fig 1.0: Clean Minimal Drupal installation

Once we have set up and logged into Drupal, you will see that its look is plain (*Fig 1.0*) and minimal, and it is a great installation profile for simple websites that don't require much functionality.

This usually tends to be when we decouple Drupal or make it *headless*, which is another popular term used. We will cover this in the last chapter.

You will also notice that there is no navigation. To get to our modules page, either go to `/admin/modules` or click **Administration** and then click **Extend**.

It's so plain here. In fact, we only get 10 modules enabled. They are as follows:

- Block
- Database Logging
- Field
- Filter
- Node
- System
- User
- Text

These are modules needed for Drupal to run, and they cannot be disabled.

To continue the development of our events website, we need to enable the following:

- Core:
    - Automated Cron
    - CKEditor
    - Contextual Links
    - Configuration Manager
    - Field UI
    - Path
    - Menu UI
    - Statistics
    - Syslog
    - Taxonomy
    - Text Editor
    - Toolbar
    - Update Manager
    - Views
    - Views UI

- Field types:
    - Datetime
    - File
    - Options

Some required modules must be enabled

- You must enable the History, Comment modules to install Forum.

Would you like to continue with the above?

Continue Cancel

 If you enable a module and it has a dependency of another module, then a message will show, as seen in the preceding image.

So, now, we have the modules we want enabled (note, these are just core modules)

Then, we can continue with setting up our event website. First off, let's just enable Seven theme or Bootstrap.

Creating our user roles

For this website, we will create two new user roles:

- **Speaker**: They will have access to create a session and edit their session
- **Organizer**: They will have access to create event-specific content, assign sessions to day, timeslots, and track skill and the status of the session.

Creating our session

Now that we have a better look, let's start by creating our content type for sessions.

Once here, add a new content type, calling it **Session** and the description **A session submitted by an authenticated user**.

Change **Title field label** to **Session name** and then save this content type.

What we will need to do is create several taxonomies.

Time and date

We will create two taxonomies for this. Our first will be time and our second day. This is how the sessions will be organised.

Room

We will have one taxonomy for this, where we will use the taxonomy name for the name of our room. However, we can add additional fields to our room to have photos, capacity, and any other fields we require.

Skill level

We will have a taxonomy set up for this that will show the type of skills needed. Again, this will use the taxonomy name.

Tracks

We will have a taxonomy set up for this and keep it simple using the taxonomy name.

Now, we have our taxonomies created we can create our session content type. To do this, we will need the following:

- Session description
- Time and date
- Room
- Track
- Skills
- Slides upload
- Selection status

As our session will be *categorized* to sort in the schedule; we will use taxonomy references. By default, there are some fields we don't want specific users to access. To restrict these fields to a specific user role, we will use **Field permissions** (https://drupal.org/project/field_permissions).

What this lets us do is allow certain user roles the ability to set whether the field can be created, edited, or viewed. This is a simple way that means we don't need to do any custom code to target these fields and it means that we can use it anywhere in our website and not require additional development. Of course, the great power of the configuration manager in Drupal 8 means all this configuration can be exported.

Now, the Field permissions is enabled. Let's start adding our fields for our session.

Entity reference fields

As we have created our taxonomy vocabularies, we will need to allow the values to be referenced. The reasons we are doing it this way are as follows:

1. Once there is data in a list field type, we cannot change the key or value of this without writing custom code. This is because all the information that is needed by Drupal for the field is stored here and, once data exists for this field, then it cannot be changed.
2. We want to categorize our content and have an interface that our admin users can easily add values for and, by using entity reference types, we are doing what relational databases do, which is have an ID, look up that ID elsewhere, and access the data associated to that ID.

Now that we understand what we want to achieve, let's make it happen.

We want our session to have our referenced data, so let's create our Time of our session. As we're using a taxonomy for this, we will only allow a list of times to be selected and restrict the creation to our taxonomy page.

Create a new field of the type **Taxonomy term** and give it a label of **Time**. Then, leave the **Field settings** as they are set and click the **Save field settings**. On the next page, we will target the taxonomy vocabulary to reference.

For this, we want to select **Time**. Of course, if we wanted for some reason to choose multiple, then we would have a selector to pick the vocabulary on our form, as all we are doing is referencing an entity type and its bundle(s) to get a taxonomy id, so the value stored in our field is the entity ID. In this case, it's our `tid`.

Now, create a field for the day using a taxonomy term for the type of reference, keeping the number of values to 1 and then clicking **Save field settings** next. We want to make our **Date vocabulary** available to the field reference. Click **Save settings**.

Repeat this for **Room**, **Track**, and **Skills**, and create a field that references these individual taxonomy vocabularies, so each field is referencing its required vocabulary. Once this is done, we will add some more fields, but these fields will be specific to the session.

Now, we will create a session status field, which will be a **List (integer)** field. We want to add the following values: **Accepted**, **Declined**, and **Pending**.

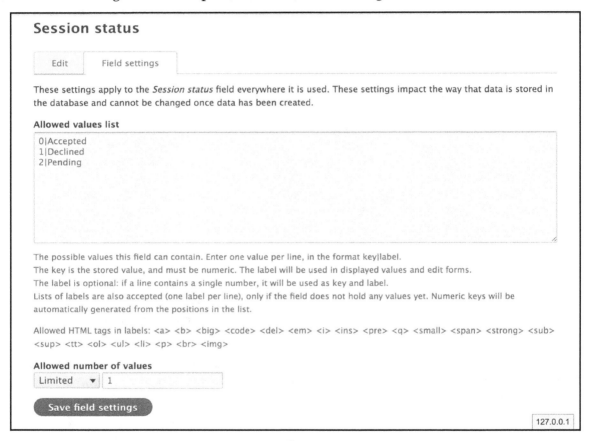

Fig 1.1: Generated keys for list field

As we can see in *Fig 1.1*, Drupal has generated a numeric key for each value. When this type of field is selected, the key will be stored as the value for the field.

We now need to add our file upload for the slides and we will be done with our session field creation for the time being. Let's call our field slides and click **Save field settings**. We will then add additional field extensions of pdf, docx, doc, ppt, pptx, and key.

Great stuff! We have the fields we require for our session creation, but currently, any authenticated user can fill the session form and fields out that we might not want our speakers to edit.

Restricting fields

If we wanted to hide fields from users, we could simply just drag them into the **Disabled** fields on **Manage form display** and **Manage display** for our content type. However, we want to do this for our user role of **organizer**.

To administer the field permissions, we need to edit the field, so let's start off by editing the **Day**. This page will look familiar; however, you will notice there is a new section called **Field visibility and permissions**.

There are three options for this:

- **Public**: Anyone can edit and view this field
- **Private**: Only author and admin can view this field and its value
- **Custom**: Specific user roles can view, add, or edit the field value

Field visibility and permissions

○ Public
    Author and administrators can edit, everyone can view.
○ Private
    Only author and administrators can edit and view.
◉ Custom permissions
    Define custom permissions for this field.

These permissions apply to all instances of this field.

PERMISSION	ANONYMOUS	AUTHENTICATED	SPEAKER	ORAGANIZER
Create own value for field field_day	○	○	○	○
Edit own value for field field_day	○	○	○	○
Edit anyone's value for field field_day	○	○	○	○
View own value for field field_day	○	○	○	○
View anyone's value for field field_day	○	○	○	○

Fig 1.2: Custom permission for field

In *Fig 1.2*, we can see a similar matrix to what we have on our global permissions page.

For this field, we only want the organizer to be able to do anything, so check all the checkboxes in the **ORGANIZER** column. Once this is done, click **Save settings**.

We will repeat this step as we have done in *Fig 1.3* for the other fields. Now, let's amend our fields and how they are displayed inside our node edit form. Change all the field widgets for our referenced fields to **Select list**.

Of course, if you want to change the layout of the form, you can enable **Field group** as we previously did and split it up to how you want.

As we have now set some permissions for our **Day** field, which will only show to the organizer the user role and allow them to add, edit, or delete the field value, we will create a session to demonstrate this.

We will populate all our taxonomy vocabularies we have created with values that we want to show on our session content type form.

Once we have done this in our session content type, we have our various fields that reference our taxonomy vocabularies.

We can leave the taxonomy term reference fields empty because part of the organizer role is to assign the taxonomies to the fields after the session submission has closed and they are selecting the sessions.

By just filling in the **Session name**, **Description**, and for now, selecting **Saturday** as our day, we can save our session and, as an anonymous user, view what the session has.

---

test session

Submitted by admin on Fri, 06/23/2017 - 23:34
Day
Saturday 3rd March 2018

Fig 1.3: Session being viewed by anonymous user

In *Fig 1.3*, we can see the fields being shown are just the **Session name** and the **Day** that the session is on. However, we cannot see any other fields. This is because the permissions of this field are just for **Day** to display. For us to change this, we must go back to each field and amend the permissions.

PERMISSION	ANONYMOUS	AUTHENTICATED	SPEAKER	ORAGANIZER
Create own value for field field_day	☐	☐	☐	☑
Edit own value for field field_day	☐	☐	☐	☑
Edit anyone's value for field field_day	☐	☐	☐	☑
View own value for field field_day	☐	☐	☐	☑
View anyone's value for field field_day	☑	☑	✓	✓

Fig 1.4: Field permission matrix

In *Fig 1.4*, we have set the field to be viewable by all the user roles but only the organizer role can do any actions on the field.

However, for the fields that the author of the session can add to, which are as follows, will be viewable by all user roles:

- Body
- Skills
- Slides
- Track

However, they will only be editable by the author and a speaker/admin.

PERMISSION	ANONYMOUS	AUTHENTICATED	SPEAKER	ORAGANIZER
Create own value for field body	☐	☑	✓	✓
Edit own value for field body	☐	☑	✓	✓
Edit anyone's value for field body	☐	☐	☐	☑
View own value for field body	☐	☑	✓	✓
View anyone's value for field body	☑	☑	✓	✓

Fig 1.5: Field permission matrix for user editable fields

In *Fig 1.5*, we can see the permissions we will need for a field that the author can modify. This needs to be repeated for any other fields we want our author to modify.

Once we have done this, we need to populate our taxonomies and then we can view the form as an admin user role. Of course, we will add all the user functionality in after this.

Go to **Admin** | **Structure** | **Taxonomy** and, for each taxonomy, populate with some data that is relevant for each. For the time, set the names to be **HH:MM--HH:MM**. This way, when we do our session schedule display later, we have our time all set out for us.

If we then go and create a session content type as an admin user, we will see all the fields listed and the taxonomy reference fields, each populated with our taxonomies. However, when we login as a new user, we will see a few fields.

Managing permissions

First, we need to set some permissions for our authenticated and speaker user roles. To do this, we need to go to our user permissions page **Admin** | **People** | **Permissions**.

If you go down to **Field Permissions**, you will see all the fields that we changed when we were editing our fields earlier on. All it was doing in the edit field section was making it easier to manage the permissions, but if you change them here, then they will change the field and how its settings are when the field is edited.

Next, we want our authenticated and speaker user roles to be able to create, edit, and delete their sessions. In order to do this, we need to set permissions for our **Session** content type.

PERMISSION	ANONYMOUS USER	AUTHENTICATED USER	SPEAKER	ORAGANIZER
View published content	☑	☑	✓	✓
Session: Create new content	☐	☑	✓	✓
Session: Delete any content	☐	☐	☐	☐
Session: Delete own content	☐	☐	☐	☐
Session: Delete revisions Role requires permission to *view revisions* and *delete rights* for nodes in question, or *administer nodes*.	☐	☐	☐	☐
Session: Edit any content	☐	☐	☐	☐
Session: Edit own content	☐	☑	✓	✓
Session: Revert revisions Role requires permission *view revisions* and *edit rights* for nodes in question, or *administer nodes*.	☐	☐	☐	☐
Session: View revisions	☐	☐	☐	☐

Fig 1.6: Session content type permissions

In *Fig 1.6*, we can see our permissions that we need to set for our content type. Of course, we can allow sessions to be deleted by the author, but for now, let's leave this as it is. Once this is done, head to the bottom and click **Save permissions**.

Now that our permissions are saved and updated, we need to create our users and user journey.

User dashboard

As with any of our user interaction, once logged in, we need to allow for a way to navigate around the website. So, what we will do is create a user dashboard that our logged in users are redirected to. We will be using views to do this. The dashboard will show an add **session** button at the top and then list any session beneath that this specific user has submitted.

Now, let's go to views and create our new view. For this view, we will name it **Dashboard**, giving it a path of /dashboard and setting the **Display format** to **Table** and click **Save and edit**.

Once on our page display, let's add some more fields:

- **Edit**
- **Session status**
- **Authored on**

Now, click **Add and configure fields** for our first field, change the label to **Operation** and the **Text to display** to **Edit**, and click **Apply and continue**. For the next field, leave as the default settings and click **Apply**.

Now, let's change the order of the fields order. To do this, click the down arrow that's next to **FIELDS** and then click **Rearrange**; a popup will appear that shows a drag-able table. Simply drag the **Content: Session status Session status** to be previous the **Content: Link to edit Content Operation** and click **Apply**. Now, our table will be listed benath with 1 result. Let's now add our link to the header of the view so that our users can submit a session.

Next to **Header**, click **Add** and then, with the popup, scroll down to **Unfiltered text**, select it, and click **Add and configure header**.

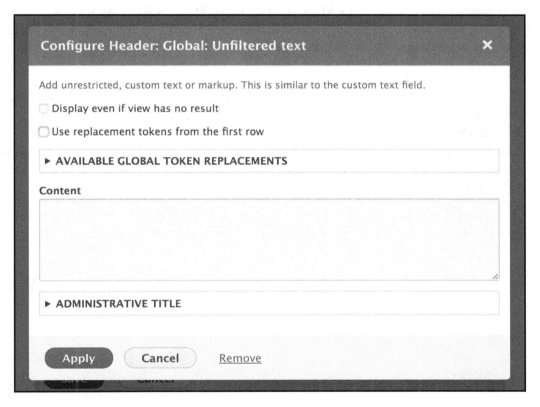

Fig 1.8: View header configuration

In *Fig 1.8*, we can see some settings for our header, as follows:

- **Display even if view has no result**: This sets our header as exactly that, a header. Whereas, by default, it will hide when no results are returned.
- **User replacement tokens from the first row**: This allows us to take a field value from our fields section in the left column.
- **Content**: This is where our content goes; this can be HTML or just plain text. However, we can use a token inside here, which is available to us by seeing the tokens we can use in **AVAILABLE GLOBAL TOKEN REPLACEMENTS**.
- For now, we are going to ignore this and click **Cancel**. Going back to our **Fields**, we are going to add a new field, click **Add**, select **Custom text** from the field list, and click **Add and configure fields**.
- Next, uncheck **Create a label** and check **Exclude from display**.
- Moving down and inside **Text**, add **Submit a session**. Preceding this, click on **Rewrite Results** and check **Output this field as a custom link**. Inside this, change Link path to /add/node/session and click **Apply**.
- So, now we have added a field that holds custom text for us to use in our header. Let's now go back to **Header** and add our field. Same as before, select **Global: Unfiltered text**.

Now, let's check **Display even if view has no result** and **Use replacement tokens from the first row**. Once we have done, this we can see tokens to use from our fields.

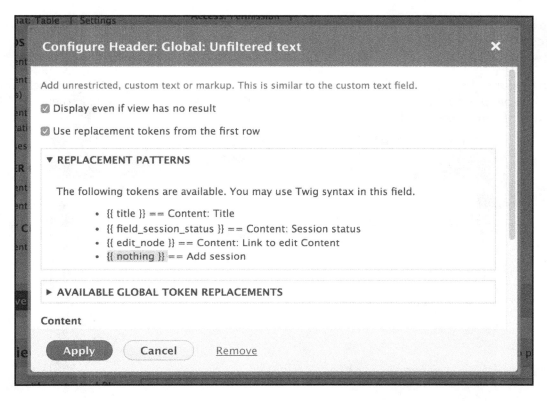

Fig 1.9: Available field tokens

In *Fig 1.9* we can see tokens available to us. Take the `{{ nothing }}` token, add it into the **Content** field, and click **Apply**. What this will do is, for authors with a session, it will appear previous the table and display their sessions submitted down. We then, however, have another issue; if there are no sessions submitted, then nothing will show. To fix this, we will add to **No Results Behavior**, click **Add**, and again, select **Unfiltered text**. Then, inside the **Content** area, we will add a message and our token.

You have not submitted any sessions yet. `Please {{ nothing }}`.

And click **Apply**.

If you go down to the **Preview**, you will see a link that we just added and our sessions listed. That's all great but it's showing the sessions for all our authors, which we don't want.

Next, we will add a contextual filter that only shows the submitted sessions by that author. We have already covered this in a previous chapter, however, we will refresh our minds now by redoing it.

On the far right-hand side column, inside **Advanced**, there is **Contextual Filters**. Click **Add** and then a popup will appear. Look for ID, select the checkbox for that row, and click **Add and configure contextual filters**.

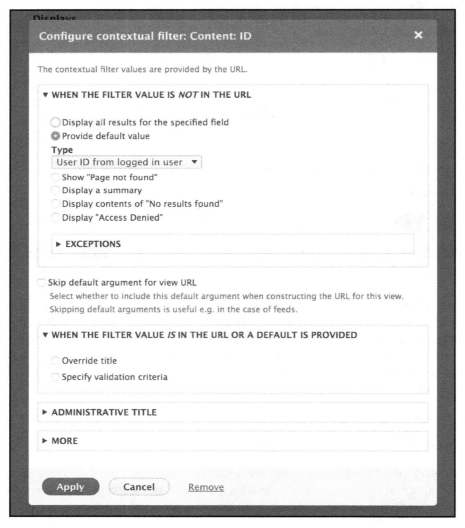

Fig 1.10: Contextual filters for ID

Once again, inside our settings for our **contextual filter** in *Fig 1.10*, we are keeping the argument basic by only providing a default value based off the logged in user, which will only show content they have authored and only show that content to them. Now, click **Apply**. As we are the author of the content, we will see it down.

The next step is to set this page to only be shown to the user roles of **Authenticated Users**.

In the middle column, under **Access**, click **Permission**, as we want to change this to a user role.

 If we wanted to create a custom permission, we would just do this inside our module inside modulename.permissions.yml and it would appear as a permission available to Drupal. Or you can add new roles through the UI admin/people/roles.

So, if we click on **Permission**, then inside the popup, change the selection to **Role** and then check **Authenticated user**.

What this means is if we were to access this page as an anonymous user, we would get redirected to an **Access Denied** error page.

User creation

When a user visits our website, we want them to be able to register and, from the registration process, we want them to be able to log in and straight away submit a session.

We will now look at setting out a user journey for after the user has registered. When the user logs in, we want them to be redirected to our /dashboard page, which means we can either use a contrib module (https://drupal.org/project) or write some custom code using hook_form_FORM_ID_alter and a submit handler.

Once this module is downloaded and enabled, go to **Admin** | **Structure** | **User default page**.

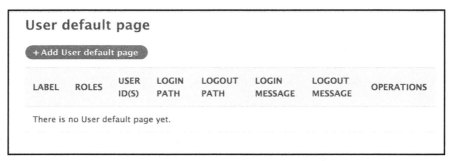

Fig 1.11: User default page

As can be seen in *Fig 1.11*, our **User default page** has a familiar table, which will list all the "rules" we require to redirect a specific user, whether it's a user role or `uid`. What we can do with this in turn is also set a rule for where the user goes when they log in and then again for when they log out, as well as the ability to display a message to the user.

For us to do this, we need to create this rule, so we need to click **+ Add User default page**. This will then take us to a configuration form for our rule, which we can now set out all the configuration we need for our user journey.

- **Label**: This is a way to know what the rule is
- **User/Role:**
    - **User/Roles**: This allows multiple user roles to be chosen
    - **Select user**: This allows us to specify a specific user
- **Login:**
    - **Redirect to URL**: The path the user is redirected to upon logging in
    - **Message**: The message that displays in our **Message** region
- **Logout:**
    - **Redirect to URL**: The path the user is redirected to upon logging in
    - **Message**: The message that displays in our **Message** region

Now, to create our own rule that will redirect all the authenticated users (for now) to our dashboard page we created earlier, do as follows:

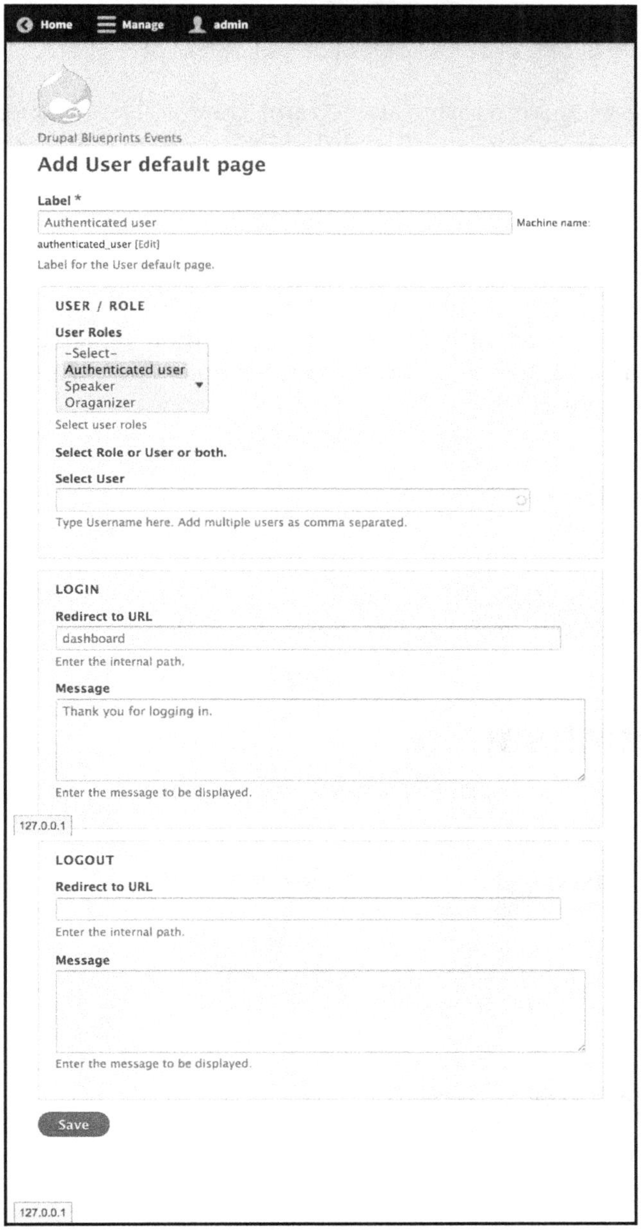

Fig 1.12: User login configuration

In *Fig 1.12*, we have filled our configuration out for what we want Drupal to action upon our users logging in.

So now, once our users logs or registers an account, they will be redirected to `/dashboard`. They can now navigate from here to what parts of the website they need access to as an authenticated user.

User fields

As we have now got our user redirection set up, we need to create our additional user fields. For this, we will add the following fields (of course, this is your website, so you can add whatever fields you want):

- `Drupal.org username`
- **Company name**
- **Position**

This will allow us to show other attendees who we are. This usually is used for networking, but it also lets us have analytics of our attendees.

Session submissions

When our authenticated user submits a session, we want to add them as a **Speaker** user role.

To do this, we will be creating a new but simple module that will upon user submission, if they have a user role only of the authenticated user and as they are logged in already, add a new role to the user of the **Speaker**.

Start by creating a new module called `event_session`.

event_speaker.info.yml

```
name: Event speaker
description: Enhances the speaker user functionality.
core: 8.x
type: module
package: Event
```

event_speaker.module

```php
<?php
/**
 * @file
 * Event speaker modifications.
 */

use Drupal\Core\Form\FormStateInterface;

/**
 * Implements hook_form_FORM_ID_alter().
 */
function event_speaker_form_node_session_form_alter(&$form,
FormStateInterface $form_state, $form_id)
{
        $form['actions']['submit']['#submit'][] =
        'event_speaker_add_role';
}

/**
 * Custom submit handler to add speaker role.
 */
function event_speaker_add_role(array $form, FormStateInterface
$form_state)
{
        $user = \Drupal::currentUser()->id();
        $user->addRole('Speaker');
}
```

Session management

Now, with our session being submitted successfully, we want to show all the sessions submitted based off their status. To do this, we will need to go back to our dashboard view we created, and add a new page display. Change the **Display name** to **Admin session management**. Then, click on **Path**, change that to /admin/sessions, and click **Apply**.

Under **Access**, click on **Authenticated user** and change to **Organizer**.

Now, we want to tidy up **Header** and **No Results Behavior**, so click on **Global: Unfiltered text (Global: Unfiltered text)** and make sure you change **For** to **This page (override)**, as otherwise, it will make this change to all our displays in this view.

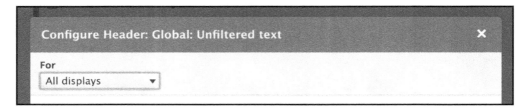

Then, click **Remove** and repeat the same for **No Results Behavior**. After this is done, move **to Contextual filters** and remove this filter, again ensuring your change **For**.

So, now we have done all this, let's add an exposed filter for to allow our organizer role to filter our submitted sessions.

We will add two filters:

- **Session status**
- **Track**
- **Day**
- Again, changing **For**.

Now that these sessions are added, we need to add a new rule for our **User default pages**. This time, we want to add a new.

- First, let's start by creating our new role. Go to **Admin | Structure | User default page** and click **+ Add User default page**.
- Set the User role to be **Organizer** and add the **Login Redirect to URL** path to be /admin/sessions and click **Save**. We won't need to edit our previous rule because our user role for **Organizer** is of a higher level.

Session display

We will create a simple view that shows our scheduled sessions in a grid in time order.

So, create a new view and give it a name of **Schedule**. Then, select **Create a page**, change **Display format** to **Grid** of **fields**, and click **Save and edit**.

Now, we need to add some fields to our view:

- **Time (hidden)**
- **Title**
- **Room (hidden)**

We will also want to show the authors the Drupal.org username. So, to do this, we need to create a relationship to users entity type. When we do this, we have access to all the components needed by user entity type.

To do this, click on **Relationships** in the far right column and click **Add**. Then, look for **User** on the field list and click **Apply**. Now, we have access to our user entity type components.

Add our field for **User** and then add another field. In the search box, type the fieldname. In this case, it's Drupal.org username and then select this.

Now, we can see our authors `Drupal.org username`. As we now have our fields listed, we want to set out our display for the fields. Next, to Format, click on **Settings** and a popup will appear.

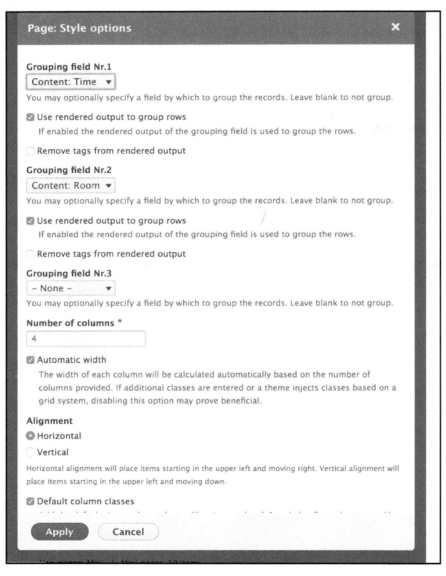

Fig 1.13: Style options

In *Fig 1.13*, we can see that we have **Grouping field Nr.1**, **Grouping field Nr.2**, and **Grouping field Nr.3**.

As we have three fields added, we can use these fields to group our rows. For ours, we only want to group two rows. Once the fields are selected, click **Apply**.

Now, we can view our schedule in the following preview, we can then click **Save** and then go to /schedule.

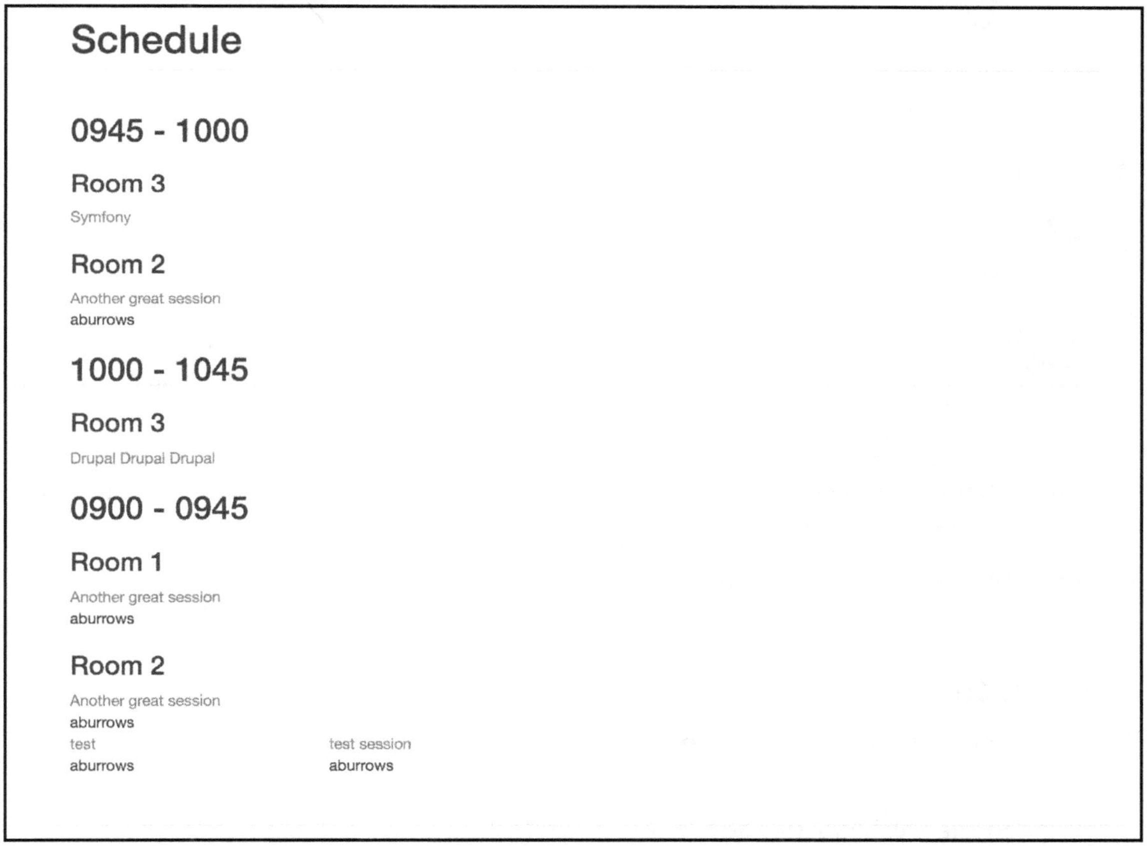

Schedule

0945 - 1000

Room 3

Symfony

Room 2

Another great session
aburrows

1000 - 1045

Room 3

Drupal Drupal Drupal

0900 - 0945

Room 1

Another great session
aburrows

Room 2

Another great session
aburrows

test	test session
aburrows	aburrows

Fig 1.14: Schedule page

As can be seen in *Fig 1.14*, we can now see our **Schedule** page that shows our sessions spread out by the times and rooms we created.

Session sharing

For this, we will use the contrib module **ShareThis** (`https://drupal.org/project/sharethis`). Once this is enabled, we need to go to **Configuration**, so go to **Admin |** **Configuration** and then click on **ShareThis**.

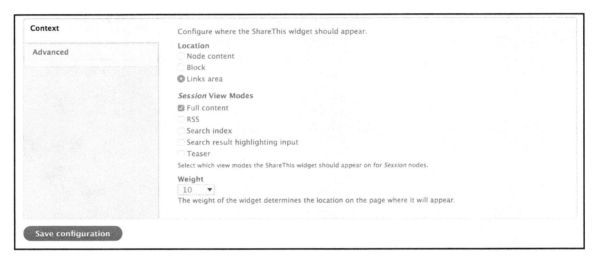

Content type location configuration

Once at the bottom of the page, we need to set where our buttons will appear. Select **Links area** and then select **Full content**.

This will now mean our share buttons will appear at the bottom of our content.

Attendees

We will create a simple view that shows our attendees in a grid, and we can search our attendees by their name.

Create a new view called **Attendees** and change the **Show Content** to be **Users**. This is because we want our view to have access to all our user entity fields.

Next, select **Create a page** and click **Save and edit**.

Now, we can add to our view. Notice that we don't need to use a relationship for our user details because we are already accessing our user entity type. All we need to do now is add the following:

- `User: Name`
- `User: Drupal.org username`

Now we just created a view that shows user data in a grid. If you want, you can add all sorts of sorting and filters. But we will keep outs simple for this.

Summary

In this chapter, we have used our previous knowledge to build an event website using mostly Drupal 8.x core but also a few contrib modules (far fewer than the previous Drupal core versions) and one custom module.

We have looked at limiting field access to specific user roles. This will then give us greater control on who can do what, but also, it allows us to have all the fields we require in our entity types and not need to create a load of rules for them. This also means no need to use `hook_form_alter()`, which is easier for website builders.

Next, we moved onto user registration, again using our previous knowledge but also adding rules to what happens when a certain user logs in.

We added a custom rule in the code to our node creation form for our session submission so that our user can be added as a **Speaker** role.

You will have noticed how powerful Drupal 8.x core is, and how little our modifications have been. This allows us to build powerful websites and indeed systems very easily, and then, if we need to enhance it any more, we can make our custom modules to extend Drupal core.

Now we will move onto creating a website that shows videos and explores panels to display our content, with different ways to display show content and show based off a specific selection criteria.

7
Get Teaching with Drupal

These types of websites are appearing more and more, and are used to help people and potentially make money.

The basic functionality of this website is to allow a way to teach others how to do certain tasks, such as teaching someone how to fix a car.

In this chapter, we will build a website that allows a registered user to view videos of tutorials. For the videos, we will use sessions from Drupalcamp London YouTube channel, but of course, you can use your own.

You will be able to create taxonomies and tag videos to those taxonomies so that a list of videos in those categories will show up.

We will look at using Panels (`https://drupal.org/project/panels`) to do our layouts on our pages.

Getting started

So once again, get a clean installation set up and let's get ready to go.

 Throughout this chapter, there are a lot of aspects we have already covered. If you are unsure of how to create a content type for example, please review in a previous chapter.

Categorizing our Lessons

Before we can create our Lessons, we need to set up our taxonomy vocabulary, so let's go to Taxonomy and create a new vocabulary called **Lesson type**.

Start by creating a new content type and let's call this **Lesson**. In our Lesson, we will want to allow our administrator to add a Lesson video, description, and taxonomy.

Video embed

For our video, we will use a contrib module called **Video Embed Field** (`https://drupal.org/project/video_embed_field`). Let's add this to our `composer` file.

Now that we have downloaded `video_embed_field`, let's enable it. What this does is it creates a new field type that is available for any entity type.

Start off by adding a new field and then selecting **Video Embed**. Then, fill the label in as `Lesson video` and click **Save and continue**. Then, on the next page, click **Save and continue** and then we are shown the **Settings** for the field.

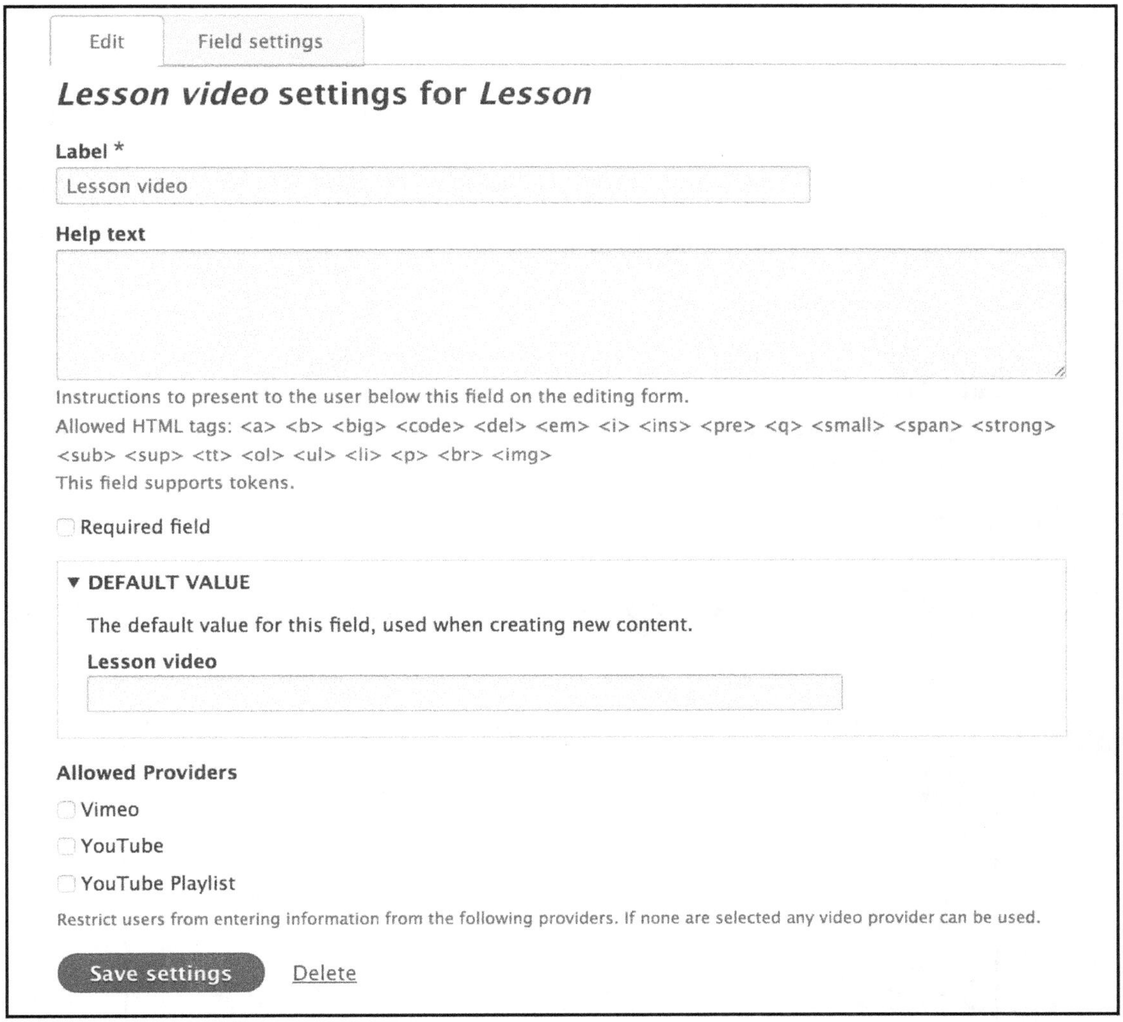

| Edit | Field settings |

Lesson video settings for *Lesson*

Label *

Lesson video

Help text

Instructions to present to the user below this field on the editing form.
Allowed HTML tags: <a> <b> <big> <code> <del> <em> <i> <ins> <pre> <q> <small> <span> <strong> <sub> <sup> <tt> <ol> <ul> <li> <p>
 <img>
This field supports tokens.

☐ Required field

▼ DEFAULT VALUE

The default value for this field, used when creating new content.

Lesson video

Allowed Providers

☐ Vimeo

☐ YouTube

☐ YouTube Playlist

Restrict users from entering information from the following providers. If none are selected any video provider can be used.

Save settings   Delete

Fig 1.0: Video embed field settings

In *Fig 1.0,* we can see we have the base 2 video providers. Of course, there are more available as extra modules or you can create your own additional one as a module. Select **YouTube** and click **Save settings**. Once we have done this, let's go straight to **Manage display** and see what our **Lesson video** is giving us for our display.

By default, we get two choices of Format:

- Thumbnail
- Video

With thumbnail, we can choose a thumbnail for the video and link it to content or an external URL. Ideally, we don't want to do this, as we want to display our video on our page. So, instead of that, we will select **Video**.

What we now get is two settings:

- **Autoplay** : This will play the video when our user role doesn't have the **never autoplay videos** permission
- **Responsive video**: This will make the video respond to the size of its container and then the size of the screen

Now that we have our video field set up, let's quickly add a YouTube video link to a new Lesson node and see what we get.

You will notice that we have a textfield for our video. All that needs to go here is the **Share** URL that is on the YouTube video.

Fig 1.1: YouTube share video

Just copy and paste this into the **Lesson video** field and then click **Save and keep published**.

Now, you can see we have our simple body content and video on display.

We can add our description field; this is going to be a long text field. Give this field a name of Lesson plan and then, after this field is created, let's create our Lesson category field, which is a **Reference type** field of taxonomy.

Inside the **Settings** for our **Reference type** field, we will select our taxonomy vocabulary of **Lesson type** and then save the field.

So now that we have set up our fields for our **Lesson**, let's add some content.

Using Panels

Just like Display Suite, Panels allows website builders the ability to layout their content into columns; it can change the layout based off certain rules.

For example, on a content page, I want to change the layout based off a certain user role. This can all be done using Panels.

Panels is one of my favourite modules, as it makes setting out layouts so simple. We can, of course, create our own layouts as well.

To get Panels, simply type `composer require drupal/panels drupal/page_manager`.

What we have just downloaded is the core Panels module and Page Manager.

Page Manager is what allows us to modify our contents layouts; by default, we have several layouts in Panels, and of course, we can add more inside our theme.

We need to enable Panels, IPE, and Page Manager. You would also have noticed that Chaos Tools (`https://drupal.org/project/ctools`) is also downloaded as it's a dependency of panels. In the previous versions of Drupal, ctools was required by Views, Panels, Panelizer, and some other popular contrib modules. We will go into more detail about panels and its associated modules as we continue on in this chapter.

Now, we need to enable the following:

- Panels
- Panels IPE
- Page Manager
- Page Manager UI

Once we have enabled these Panels modules, we will create a two-column layout for our Lessons.

To do this, we need to go to the **Panels configuration**. This is located inside **Structure**, so go to **Admin | Structure** and then click on **Pages**.

So, once we are on the **Pages configuration** page, we can see **Node view** in our table. What this is doing is now using Panels to control how our nodes are rendered. By default, it's enabled and allows us to modify the output of our nodes. As we want to change the layout of our **Lesson**, let's go and edit this. We then are shown another page of **Settings** with a side column of menu items and a main content area.

As we want to change only the layout for our **Lesson** content type, we need to create a variant of our **Panel Settings**. This will clone what we have already and allow us to target our specific content types, assign different layouts, and show different content all based off access-based rules we can configure.

Using variants

At the top left, click **Add variant**. We will then see a popup that has a configuration that we can add our **Settings** for our new variant.

- **Label**: This is what we will call our variant, and is what we are shown when editing our panel
- **Type**: This is the type of variant we will create
- **HTTP status code**: This is based off a typical HTTP status code, for example: **404 page not found**, **403 access denied**, and **301 page redirect**
- **Optional features**: These features enhance our variant, and give us greater control on access to our variant

As we want to create our Panel using the Page Manager, we will choose **Panels** from **Type**. This will allow us to use the Panels functionality. We also want this variant to only be set for our **Lesson** content type, so we will select **Selection criteria**. Now, click **Save**.

As we selected **Selection criteria**, we will be taken to configuration for this. There is a table that lists all the criteria we have added. Preceding the table is a dropdown that has multiple options that allows us to choose what type of criteria it is, as follows:

- **Content type**
- **Node bundle**
- **Current theme**
- **Request path**
- **User role**

For our **Lesson**, we want to set the content type for **Lesson**. We will later add an additional setting for our user to restrict the content.

Fig 1.2: Selection criteria

In *Fig 1.2*, with **Content type** selected from our dropdown, click **Add Condition** and then we will see a popup box. We want to select our **Lesson** content type and click **Save**. Once it adds to the table, click **Next**. We then have a drop-down list of **Builder**. Then, select **Standard** and click **Next**.

What we now will see is another page of configuration, as we want to have our Panel variant to show for our **Lesson** content type. This is the default page for Panels when wanting to add block or fields to our panel.

For us to add a field from our content type, click **+ Add new block**.

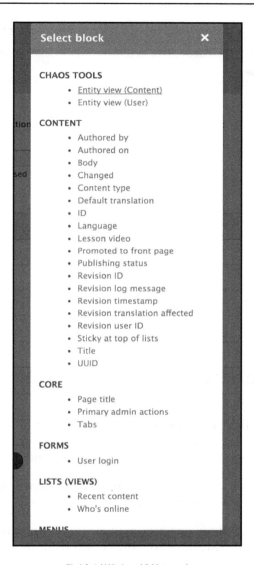

Fig 1.3: Add blocks and fields to panel

In *Fig 1.3*, we can see all the blocks we can add. Notice how, for our node type panel, we have an entire section for **Content**. This allows us to add fields to our panel.

For now, let's just add our **Lesson video** field.

Once we click on the **Lesson video** link, we are then shown some more **Settings**:

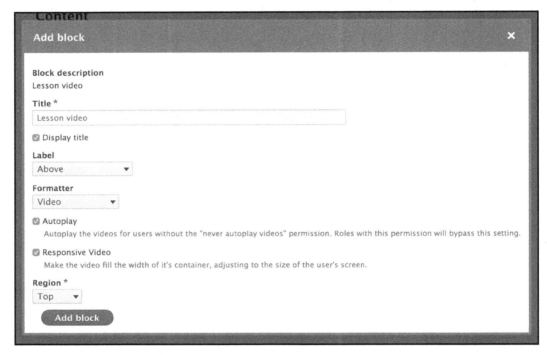

Fig 1.4: Block field settings

Notice how, in *Fig 1.4*, we have our **Manage fields** settings from earlier and a **Title** and **Display Title** from our block layout plugin. We also have a **Region** dropdown. However, this is not for our themes regions. This is for our Panel regions.

Once we click **Add block**, we then see that it adds this into our region. However, if we decide we want to move it down into another region, then we can just drag and drop it.

Now if we click **Finish**, we will see our original **Settings** page when we first started to create our Panel, and **Lesson** will show now on the left column.

If we click on **Lesson**, we will see a menu open with some menu items:

- **General**: This has the label for our variant and the type of Builder we are using. This is what we set earlier on when we were creating our variant.
- **Contexts**: This gives us extra conditions to utilize, for example, if we want to take values from our user, then we can access these objects. It works like Relationships in views.
- **Selection criteria**: This was what we set previously.

- **Layout**: This allows us to choose what layout we want to have for our variant.
- **Content**: We can add our content and fields to our layout here.

If we click **Update and save** and then go to our node that we created, in this case, its `node/1`, then we can see it's just our video field. This is because what we have done in Panels the plugin has overridden the default node view plugin, and therefore, allows us to view how it's been done in Panels.

Not only this, but it's only going to affect the selection criteria we chose that allows us to add new content types and either use the core Node display or create a new one for our content type and use Panels to do so.

Harnessing the power of variants

So now that we have our basic variant for the **Lesson** content type created, let's look at changing this so different user roles see different variants.

We want to have our authenticated user see our content in its entirety and we want our anonymous user to see different content, more of a teaser to what they can expect to see if they register.

For us to do this, we need to edit our variant we have just created and add a new selection criteria. So, click on our variant name and then click on **Selection criteria**. Now, we want to add a new condition, so change **Content Type** to **User Role**. What this now will let us do after clicking **Add Condition** is give us access to the conditions associated to the User entity type.

Fig 1.5

In *Fig 1.5*, we can see the options for our **User role** criteria for this variant, as we want authenticated users to see this only. Then, select **Authenticated user** and click **Save**.

Now that we have created this variant, it will only be used on the **Lesson** content type and for authenticated users. However, for anonymous users, they will see the default display for our content type.

 We can, of course, use this technique to have different layouts and content on display for different user roles.

But as we are using Panels, let's create our variants, so we have one for authenticated users and anonymous users.

First, let's go back and change the label we set for our first variant. Click on **Lesson** on the left-hand side column, then amend the label to say **Lesson (Authenticated)**, and click **Update and save**.

Now we have saved it, you will see on the left-hand side column, our new variant name of **Lesson (Authenticated)**.

As we have not got our variant done for authenticated users, let's add one for anonymous users.

For ours, we are simply going to add some simple text saying, "**You must be logged in to view this.**"

Start by creating a new variant by clicking **Add variant** in the top right corner. This will again bring up the pop up that has the variant configuration that we can add our **Settings** for this new variant.

Fill out the details again as we previously did; this time, give it a label of **Lesson (Anonymous)** a **Type: Panels** and **Optional features: Selection criteria** and click **Next**.

We again see our **Selection criteria** configuration page. We have two criterias that we need to add for this variant. These are **Content type: Lesson** and **User role: Anonymous**. After this is done, click **Next**, again select **Builder: Standard**, and click **Next**. To keep it simple, we will just use a **One column** layout, but of course, feel free to do which ever layout you want and click **Next**. Finally, we are on our Content page for our variant.

For now, we will leave this blank, as we need to create the content that is going to populate this variant, which we will do next. Click **Finish** and then, on the next page, click **Update and save**.

Open an incognito window on your browser and visit /node/1; this will show a blank page, as per what we just created in our variant. Pretty cool eh! Remember there is no custom code for this; we have done all this using Drupal 8.x core and Panels contrib module!

So now that we have said how great Drupal is, let's go and add some content to our **anonymous user video** page. To do this, we now have to use blocks for our content in Panels. If you have used the previous versions of Panels, you would be familiar with Panes. This has now been scrapped, as we have the power of the Plugin API and, therefore, can fully utilize the **Block** plugin. It also means we can have different fields for out blocks, and as well as this different layout for our block types. This will, of course, make our block types consistent and will allow for even quicker builds.

Move to our Block layout, which is **Admin | Structure | Block layout**. Once here, click on the **Custom block library** tab and create a basic block type called **Basic** and then click **Add custom block type**. You will then be taken to a **Settings** page to create your block type; fill this out and click **Save**. Now that we have created a block type (which we did in a previous chapter), go back to the sub tab of **Blocks** and click **Add custom block** and then click **Basic** from our list of block types. Now, enter a description of what we will call this block. After this, enter in our Body something along the lines of **"You must be logged in to see this Lesson"** and click **Save**.

So, now that we have created a new block with some basic content, let's go back to our Panel and add this to our variant **Admin | Structure | Pages** and then click **Edit**. Now, once here, let's edit out variant. Notice how we have two variants and in an alphabetical order.

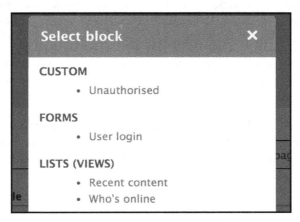

Fig 1.6: Panels select block

From here, click on **Content** and then **+ Add new block**. Then, look for a heading of custom and under that is a list of our block, as can be seen in *Fig 1.6*.

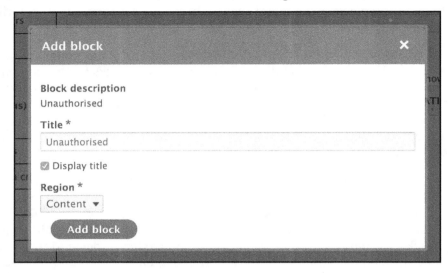

Fig 1.7: Block settings

After clicking our block name in *Fig 1.7*, we now see some **Settings** that look familiar to our block configuration and we have also seen this before in *Fig 1.5*, when we added our video to the page in our previous variant.

Now that we have added this block, we can see that it's now inside our content region for our panel and not our actual page; don't get this confused when you can't see a region from your theme here.

So now, click **Update and save**, as we don't want to lose what we have done, however Drupal temporarily does save the panel, but just be safe, and if you don't want to **Update and save** you can just save and then update later.

Great! Now that we have our two variants, let's go look as an anonymous user. What we should see is **You must be logged in to view this**. What this means is that we have now created two variants that show for our different role types. To add another variant this is just from a few bits of configuration; how awesome is this!

Organizing our Lessons

As we have now created our basic Lesson content type and are now showing two types of panel displays to our user roles, let's go and add our taxonomy vocabulary we created. Then, we will add some more videos and create a listing page for them.

So, go back to the Lesson content type and add a reference field to our taxonomy vocabulary. Once this is done, create five to ten videos in different taxonomies and then we will create a listing page for all our videos and a related video block.

Creating a listing of Lessons

With our videos, we want to allow the ability to filter and search for videos. By doing this it will make looking for the Lesson our user wants to find a lot easier.

What we want to allow our user to do is filter by taxonomy term in our case Lesson type, and then to filter it down further allow the user to use a free text search.

To do this, we need to create a view with a page display. We have previously covered how to do a filter on nodes but we are going to group and add free text for this one.

Go to views, create a new view, and call it **Available Lessons**. We want to show our nodes, so keep **Content** selected and the type of **Lesson**.

After this, select **Create a page** and give it a **Page title** of **Available Lessons** and a path `/lessons/all` and click **Save and edit**.

With our view display, we can choose to either use a view mode from our content type, as previously shown, or we can just keep it simple and use fields in the view. For this, we will keep it simple and show just the Lesson title and the Lesson video thumbnail, which is generated from the upload of the video.

Once we have added these fields, we want to then group them up based off the Lesson type. To do this, we need to add our **Lesson type** field and then **Exclude from display**. We now need to change our display format to **Grid** and click **Settings**.

Then, set **Grouping field Nr.1** to **Content: Lesson type** and click **Apply**. Now, you will see in preview our Lessons grouped by the type of Lesson.

Next, we want to add some exposed filters, so let's add **Lesson type** and some free text for the title and the Lesson description. So, let's add our Body field to it and exclude it from the view display. After doing this, in **Filter Criteria**, add a new filter called **Global: Combine fields filter** and next we want to expose the filter.

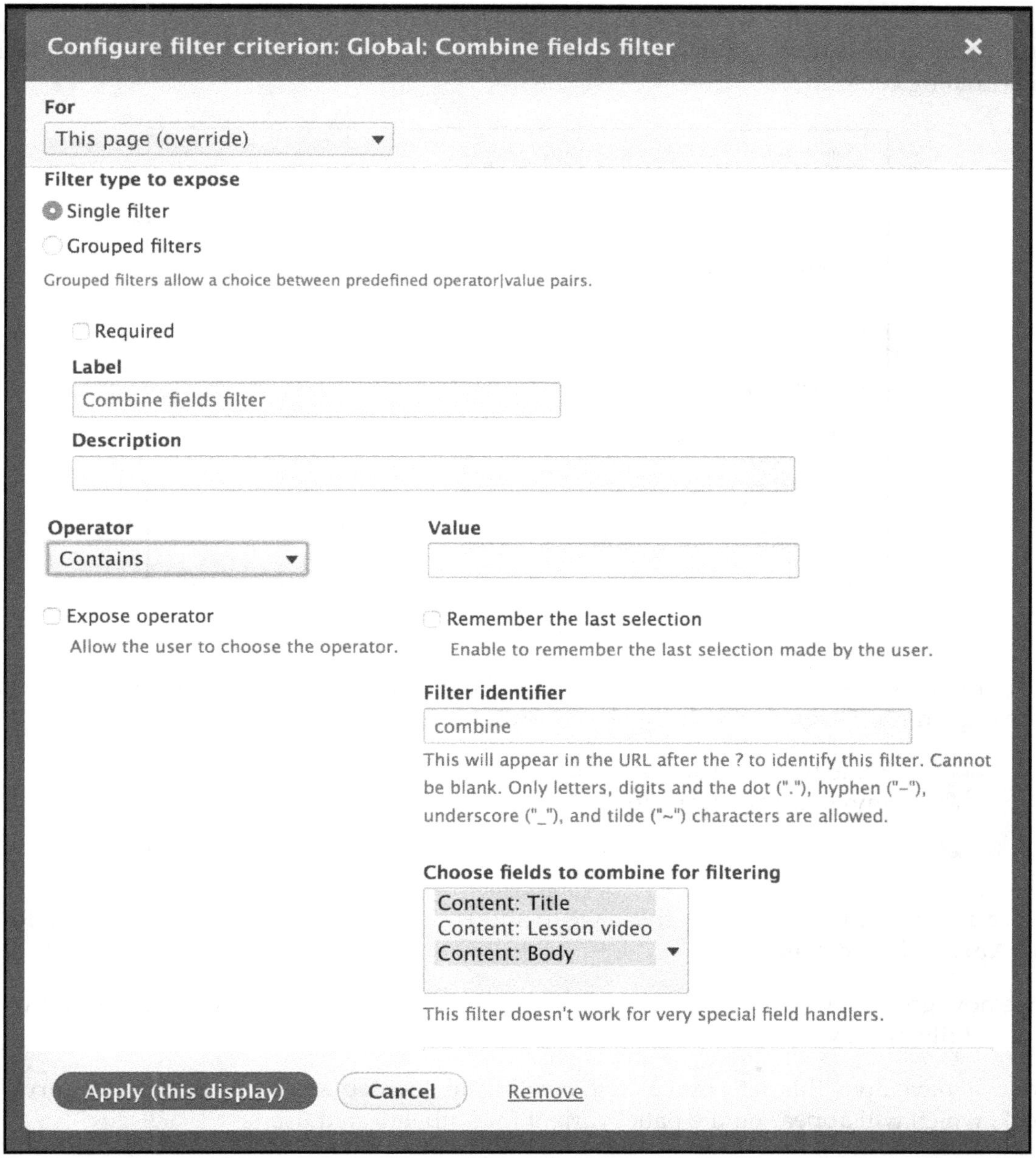

Configure filter criterion: Global: Combine fields filter   ✕

For

| This page (override)   ▼ |

Filter type to expose

◉ Single filter

◯ Grouped filters

Grouped filters allow a choice between predefined operator|value pairs.

◯ Required

Label

| Combine fields filter |

Description

| |

Operator   **Value**

| Contains   ▼ | | |

◯ Expose operator   ◯ Remember the last selection

Allow the user to choose the operator.   Enable to remember the last selection made by the user.

Filter identifier

| combine |

This will appear in the URL after the ? to identify this filter. Cannot be blank. Only letters, digits and the dot ("."), hyphen ("–"), underscore ("_"), and tilde ("~") characters are allowed.

Choose fields to combine for filtering

| Content: Title |
| Content: Lesson video |
| Content: Body   ▼ |

This filter doesn't work for very special field handlers.

(**Apply (this display)**)   (Cancel)   Remove

Fig 1.8: Combine fields filter

In *Fig 1.8*, we can see that we can select multiple fields to search within our filter. This is great because we can now search multiple fields inside our view. This is a simple approach for searching content.

Fig 1.9: Exposed filters with Combine filters

In *Fig 1.9*, we can see our combine filter is now showing any nodes with **great** in; if we were to change this to **Lorem**, we will see other results.

 Remember we can have our exposed filters as a block, so it can appear anywhere on our page.

As we are only wanting to show this page to authenticated users, change the Access to **Role** and **Authenticated user**.

If we now go to view our page, we can see that the Lessons are grouped and we have two exposed filters showing.

Now we have done this, let's move on to creating an **Available Lessons in this category** block, which will appear on the panel variant for authenticated users.

To do this, go back to the view we created and add a new view display of **Block**, and remove the filter criteria. But remember to change **All displays** to **This block (override)**, otherwise it will affect our page display.

So currently, we just have the same as our page, but without the exposed filters. However, we only want to show Lessons that are in the same category as the current Lesson we're on. So, we need to add a **contextual filter**, as the view needs to know some information from our entity in order to work out the relationship between our entities.

In **contextual filters** on the right-hand side column, click **Add** and then look for **Content: Has a taxonomy term ID**.

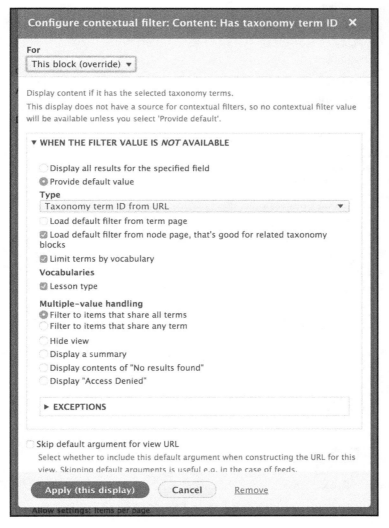

Fig 1.10: Contextual filters

In *Fig 1.10*, we can see the settings needed for our **contextual filter**. We want to provide a default value based off the ID, so we need to get the **Taxonomy term ID from URL** and then we want to show related nodes for this term. We then want to add some additional validation.

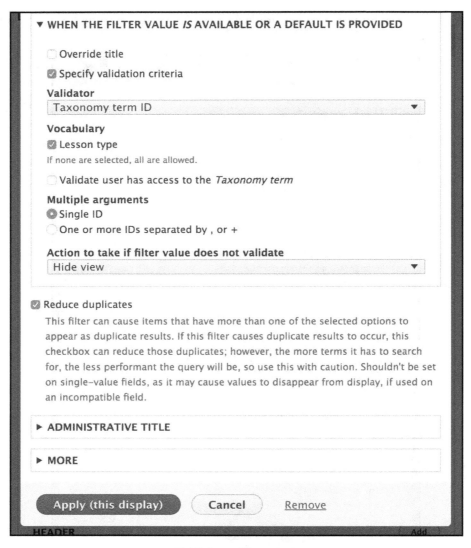

Fig 1.11: Contextual filters continued.

Moving down and into *Fig 1.11*, we can see we want to filter down our contextual filter so that it is only for our Lesson type vocabulary. Once we have done this, click **Apply (this display)**. Again, we won't see anything in our preview; this is because we have no argument in the URL to obtain our information from.

So, enter 1 and click **Update preview**.

We should see videos associated to that term ID. Now that this is done, we need to add to our **Lesson** content type, so we need to go back into Panels and edit our variant for **Lesson (Authenticated)** and then add the block we have just created anywhere on our content part of the variant.

Once this is done, click **Save and update** and then go to /node/1, and you will see our **Available Lessons** that is showing the Lesson related to our **Lesson type**.

Summary

In this chapter, we have used what we have already learned with views to create some simple filtering displays that allowed us to filter our content that we output into a grid and gave the ability to upload YouTube videos into our content.

We have used a contrib module called Panels and looked at how we can control user access and show different displays to users based off their user role, all without touching one line of code.

Finally in our last chapter we will look at decoupling Drupal and using it just to store our content, so that we can output it to a static HTML frontend.

8
Go Static with Drupal

Becoming increasingly popular, we are seeing websites and applications using a CMS like Drupal as a content management framework that outputs JSON to a static frontend using popular JavaScript Framework, such as Angular, Node, or React. For this chapter, we will look at Drupal's built-in REST API and how we can send data from Drupal to a frontend framework.

This kind of functionality is becoming used more for applications, but a lot of websites are using this to and harnessing the power of Drupal as a content management system.

We will look at using Drupal's built-in REST API and allowing our frontend to read the data and output it by covering the following topics:

- Creating our content type
- Enabling the Drupal core modules needed
- Creating our view to show our content output
- Creating our frontend using React

 This chapter will get hands on with React - https://facebook.github.io/react/.

Getting started

In order for us to start, we require to have a clean Drupal 8.x installation.

Once this is set up, we will create our content type. For this chapter, we want to show some cars on our frontend.

In Drupal 8, we have the ability to use REST within Drupal core this means we don't need to develop this functionality as its available within Drupal 8 core just by enabling a few core modules, which we will cover in this chapter.

What is REST?

When we create a web service, we want to allow applications to access that data using a web service. **REST** stands for **Representational State Transfer** and it is a way that allows a request over HTTP to be actioned, whether it's GET, POST, PUT, or DELETE.

An example of this is we have a lot of data exposed using REST and it is output to a URL into a JSON format. We can access that data by going to a URL we create; these are known as endpoints and can be any type of URL, for example, /api/cars. What we will see is data from our system formatted in JSON. We can now read this data and use it how we want.

How does it work in Drupal?

Inside Drupal, we can use the REST API to take our content and output it in a format that can be read.

First, we need to enable some modules:

- **HAL**: Serializes entities using **Hypertext Application Language**.
- **HTTP Basic Authentication**: Provides the HTTP Basic authentication provider.
- **RESTful Web Services**: Exposes entities and other resources as RESTful web API.
- **Serialization**: Provides a service for (de)serializing data to/from formats, such as JSON and XML.

Now that these modules are enabled, we will be able to create our content. So, create a new content type called cars and add the following fields:

- Car photo (image)
- Manufacturer (list)
- Model (textfield)
- Year (textfield)

Once these fields have been created, start to add some content; let's add two cars for now.

So, we now have our content. We could, of course, just build this on here, but for this chapter, we are going to use Drupal for its backend content management functionality.

Exposing Drupal using REST API

Now that we have created out two cars, we need to make them available as an endpoint. To do this is really easy in Drupal 8. We will create a new view just for our cars feed.

So, go to views and create a new view, as shown:

Fig 1.0: Create a view

You will notice there is a new setting at the bottom called **REST EXPORT SETTINGS**; this is what we are going to use to create our endpoint.

Now, give your view a name of **Cars feed** and select Content to be of type **Cars.** Select **Provide a REST export** and then give it a path; this is the path that will have our data on. Let's use /api/cars and click **Save and edit.**

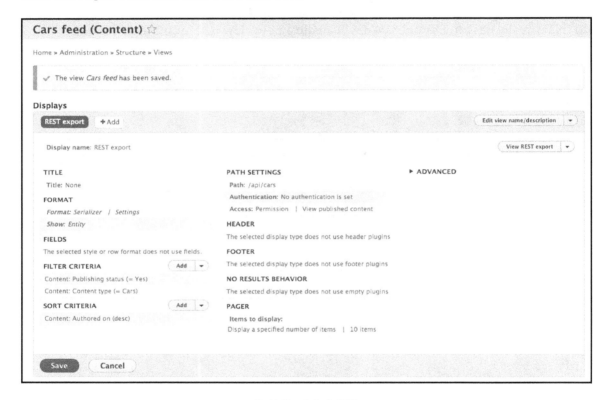

Fig 1.1: View display for REST

You will notice some differences to our view display settings in *Fig 1.1.* We only have the option to have our **Format** to be **Serializer.** This is because we need our data to be serialized. We have some settings for this format.

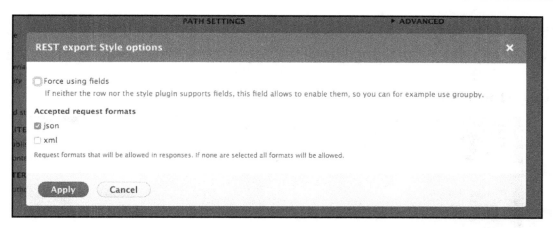

Fig 1.2: REST export format style settings

In *Fig 1.2*, we can see there are some settings that allow us to modify how our data is built. By default, the data is compiled of the entire entity object, but this can be modified to only show certain fields.

We have two formats available to us, **json** and **xml**. First let's look at our default data in the JSON format. This is without making any amends to the fields used.

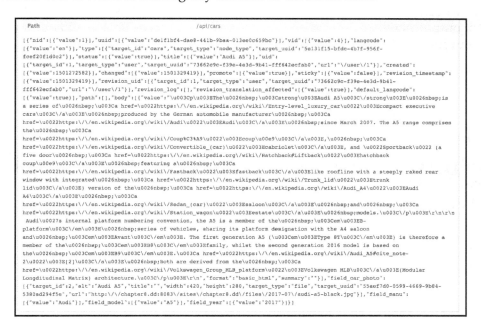

Fig 1.3: JSON output of node

As we can see, in *Fig 1.3*, the entire node is output.

So, when we access our endpoint, we will look for the data we need and return it. However, we want to keep this as simple as possible and output just the fields we need.

So, go to **Format** and change **Entity** to **Fields**.

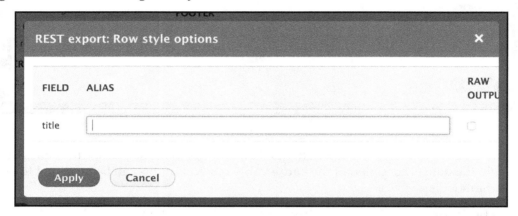

Fig 1.4: Field settings

Notice, however, in *Fig 1.4*, that we have the option to add an alias. What this will do is instead of outputting the field name in out endpoint, we will be able to add our own label to make our lives easier. We can also clean up our output, as follows:

```
[{"name":"\u003Ca href=\u0022\/node\/1\u0022
hreflang=\u0022en\u0022\u003EAudi A5\u003C\/a\u003E"}]
```

Instead of this, we will get the following:

```
[{"name":"Audi A5"}]
```

Our second option is a lot cleaner, and as we don't want to link back to our website, we don't need the URL.

For now, let's leave this as it is and add our aliases later on after we have added our fields.

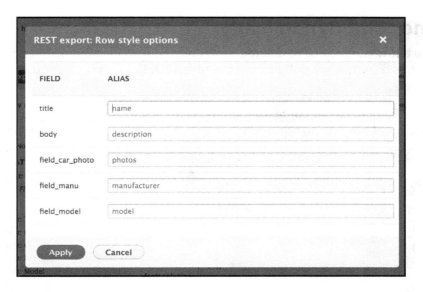

Fig 1.5: Field aliases

So now that we have added our fields aliases we can now save and view our data being output in our endpoint.

```
[{"name":"Audi A5","body":"\u003Cp\u003EThe\u00a0\u003Cstrong\u003EAudi A5\u003C\/strong\u003E\u00a0is a series
of\u00a0\u003Ca href=\u0022https:\/\/en.wikipedia.org\/wiki\/Entry-level_luxury_car\u0022\u003Ecompact
executive cars\u003C\/a\u003E\u00a0produced by the German automobile manufacturer\u00a0\u003Ca
href=\u0022https:\/\/en.wikipedia.org\/wiki\/Audi\u0022\u003EAudi\u003C\/a\u003E\u00a0since March 2007. The A5
range comprises the\u00a0\u003Ca
href=\u0022https:\/\/en.wikipedia.org\/wiki\/Coup%C3%A9\u0022\u003Ecoup\u00e9\u003C\/a\u003E,\u00a0\u003Ca
href=\u0022https:\/\/en.wikipedia.org\/wiki\/Convertible_(car)\u0022\u003Ecabriolet\u003C\/a\u003E, and
\u0022Sportback\u0022 (a five door\u00a0\u003Ca
href=\u0022https:\/\/en.wikipedia.org\/wiki\/Hatchback#Liftback\u0022\u003Ehatchback
coup\u00e9\u003C\/a\u003E\u00a0featuring a\u00a0\u003Ca
href=\u0022https:\/\/en.wikipedia.org\/wiki\/Fastback\u0022\u003Efastback\u003C\/a\u003Elike roofline with a
steeply raked rear window with integrated\u00a0\u003Ca
href=\u0022https:\/\/en.wikipedia.org\/wiki\/Trunk_lid\u0022\u003Etrunk lid\u003C\/a\u003E) version of
the\u00a0\u003Ca href=\u0022https:\/\/en.wikipedia.org\/wiki\/Audi_A4\u0022\u003EAudi
A4\u003C\/a\u003E\u00a0\u003Ca
href=\u0022https:\/\/en.wikipedia.org\/wiki\/Sedan_(car)\u0022\u003Esaloon\u003C\/a\u003E\u00a0and\u00a0\u003Ca
href=\u0022https:\/\/en.wikipedia.org\/wiki\/Station_wagon\u0022\u003Eestate\u003C\/a\u003E\u00a0models.\u003C\
/p\u003E\n\n\u003Cp\u003EUnder Audi\u0027s internal platform numbering convention, the A5 is a member of
the\u00a0\u003Cem\u003EB-platform\u003C\/em\u003E\u00a0series of vehicles, sharing its platform designation
with the A4 saloon and\u00a0\u003Cem\u003EAvant\u003C\/em\u003E. The first generation A5 (\u003Cem\u003EType
8T\u003C\/em\u003E) is therefore a member of the\u00a0\u003Cem\u003EB8\u003C\/em\u003Efamily, whilst the second
generation 2016 model is based on the\u00a0\u003Cem\u003EB9\u003C\/em\u003E.\u003Ca
href=\u0022https:\/\/en.wikipedia.org\/wiki\/Audi_A5#cite_note-2\u0022\u003E[2]\u003C\/a\u003E\u00a0Both are
derived from the\u00a0\u003Ca
href=\u0022https:\/\/en.wikipedia.org\/wiki\/Volkswagen_Group_MLB_platform\u0022\u003EVolkswagen
MLB\u003C\/a\u003E(Modular Longditudinal Matrix)
architecture.\u003C\/p\u003E","field_car_photo":"\/sites\/chapter8.dd\/files\/2017-07\/audi-a5-
black.jpg","field_manu":"Audi"}]
```

Fig 1.7: Cars endpoint

By default, we will see our cars from the feed, but what if we want to see a specific car by its ID?

Filter endpoint dynamically

If we want to allow our feed to be filtered based off arguments, then we need to use contextual filters. For this, we will filter based off an ID. But, of course, you can add more contextual filters.

So, let's add an ID field to our contextual filters. What we want to do is show all our cars by default. However, if we add an argument, we will then just see the car with that ID.

Fig 1.8: Contextual filters for car id

In *Fig 1.8*, we can see some settings for our car node ID. What we want to do is give the option of filtering by car ID. The top part allows us to filter based off ID, which will only show the cars based off that ID, for example, /api/cars/1 will return our car with that node ID.

However, if there is no car ID, then all our results will show in our endpoint.

Awesome stuff, so we now have our endpoint exposing our car nodes in a JSON format. Again, we have done no custom code whatsoever. In the face, we have no contrib modules at all. That is just how powerful Drupal 8 is in core.

So, as we have our data, we want to now create our frontend website that will show our cars on the website.

Let's go React

For this next part, we will be writing a fair bit of custom code. This is not Drupal code related it is using React JS. However, there is a prebuilt solution called Contenta CMS, which uses Drupal and some custom modules. It has a step-by-step guide on how to set a website up with it on Angular, Elm, Ember, Ionic, React, and Vue.js.

 At the time of writing this, there was no React example.

Getting ready for React

So, our React-based website will be an entirely separate website to our Drupal installation.

We won't be learning how to write React code in this; we will be using an example of some ReactJS that I have written for this. It will be explained briefly but we won't get into too much details, as this would be covered in another book.

Creating our frontend

Like any frontend application, we need to create a basic HTML page and this will the contain our JavaScript.

So, in another directory, let's create one for our React frontend to go into.

Let's call ours `react_frontend`.

Once we have created this directory, we need to create a basic HTML file:

- `index.html`

```
<!DOCTYPE html>
<html>
<head lang="en">
    <meta charset="UTF-8">
    <title>Our cars</title>
</head>
<body>
<div id="app"/>
</body>
</html>
```

Notice, however, our code is very basic indeed, as React will generate from our view ID in our `div` all our markup, as after all, it is JavaScript.

We also have only used `<div id="app"/>`; this is because our JavaScript will modify this HTML attribute based off what we put inside our code.

Next, we need to add out script tags inside `<head>`:

```
<script src="https://npmcdn.com/react@15.3.1/dist/react.js"></script>
<script
src="https://npmcdn.com/react-dom@15.3.1/dist/react-dom.js"></script>
<script src="https://unpkg.com/axios/dist/axios.min.js"></script>
<script src="https://npmcdn.com/jquery@3.1.0/dist/jquery.min.js"></script>
<script
src="https://cdnjs.cloudflare.com/ajax/libs/babel-core/5.8.24/browser.min.j
s"></script>
```

So, what we are now doing is allowing our HTML to have access to the ReactJS library and any additional components needed.

Of course, there is a much more complicated way to do this using `npm` and `https://facebook.github.io/react/` will help you with it using a step-by-step guide.

Now that we have added our basic HTML and ReactJS, we need to write some React to get this to work. To do this, we will create a new js file called `app.js` inside a directory called `js`.

Now, add the following:

- `app.js`

```
class App extends React.Component {

    constructor() {
        super();
        this.state = {
            data: []
        }
    },
    componentDidMount() {
        var t = this;
        this.serverRequest = axios.get(this.props.source)
            .then(function(event) {
                t.setState({
                    data: event.data
                });
            })
    },
    componentWillUnmount() {
        this.serverRequest.abort();
    },
    render() {
        var cars = []
        this.state.data.forEach(item => {
            cars.push(<h3 className="carname">
            {item.name[0].value}</h3> );
        })
        return (
            <div className="container">
                <div className="row">
                    <div className="col-md-12">
                        <h1 className="title">All our cars</h1>
                        {cars}
                    </div>
                </div>
            </div>
        );
    }
}

ReactDOM.render(
    <App source="https://chapter8.dd:8443/api/cars" />,
    document.getElementById('app')
);
```

Now, save this and then refresh your browser, and you should see our two car names listed:

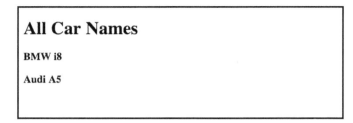

All Car Names

BMW i8

Audi A5

As we can see, in *Fig 1.9*, we have our car names listed.

The JavaScript gets the JSON data and puts it into an array. After this, it then loops through the data and gets the value for the name, in our case, name is the car brand and model. From here, it is then passed to be rendered and then it is output based off the REST API endpoint location.

Summary

Congratulations! You have just made Drupal generate data into JSON format that allows third-party systems to retrieve this data, and in our case, display the data in our frontend made in React.

Now, you can amend this to allow additional fields and amend how the styling of the page is, but this would require a more in-depth look at React.

As data is added to our feed, our output in our frontend will change and there will be nothing that is required to update our rendered content.

There are many alternatives to using React and this can either be achieved using jQuery library or there is a fantastic Drupal distribution called **Contenta CMS** (http://www. contentacms.org). I really recommend this as a great simple solution to.

There's more in core

Just as we wrap up this book, we know Drupal has REST API built into core, but what if we want to retrieve data?

Well, in Drupal, there are ways that we can do this the other way around, where by Drupal is reviewing data from an endpoint.

This again is all built into core and uses
`Symfony\Component\HttpFoundation\Request;`, which is built into Drupal 8 core.

And all this is available to be read in more detail in other Drupal 8 books.

So, if you fancy learning more on Drupal, then these books by other Packt authors are highly recommended. Especially the *Drupal 8 Cookbook*, which has been written by a very good friend of mine, Matt Glaman.

One last thing

With Drupal being an open source project, it constantly requires some love. So, on `Drupal.org`, there is an issue queue that lists any current issues with Drupal. These can range from bugs or feature requests.

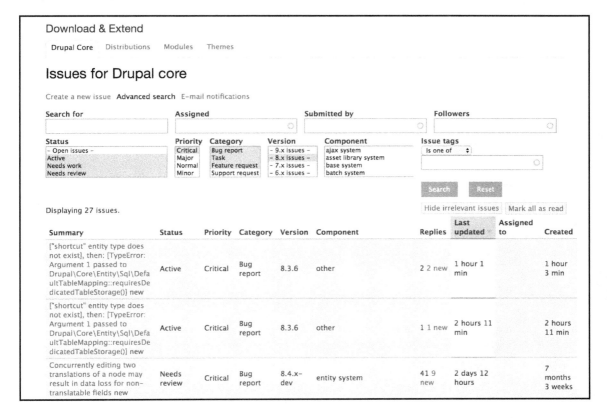

Obviously, I don't expect you to tackle a really complicated issue straight away, however, there are other issues that can be fixed like document amends, for example, there may be a request to amend some text in the code; this is a great way to get contributing to Drupal.

 There is regular communication in Drupal online.
We have irc channel(s)--*#drupal-support*, *#drupal-contribute*, and *#drupalmentoring*, and then on top of that, we also have a slack workspace, which is `drupal.slack.com`, and it offers channels for Drupal-related questions and contribution help.

Index

www.ingramcontent.com/pod-product-compliance
Lightning Source LLC
Chambersburg PA
CBHW080634060326

40690CB00021B/4930